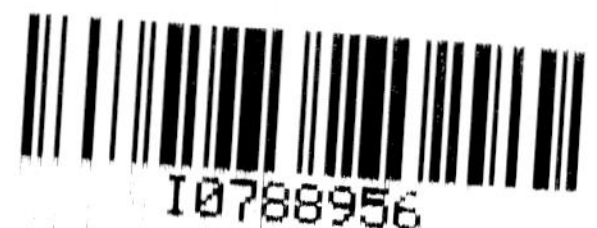

Coloring book for adults and kids amazing horse image for design

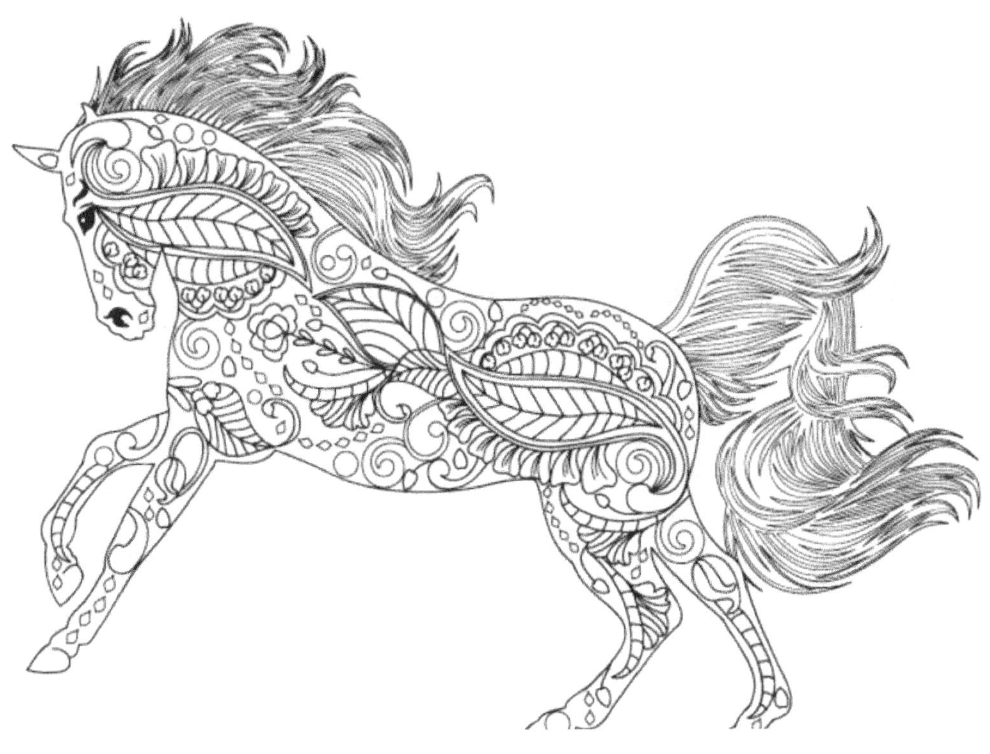

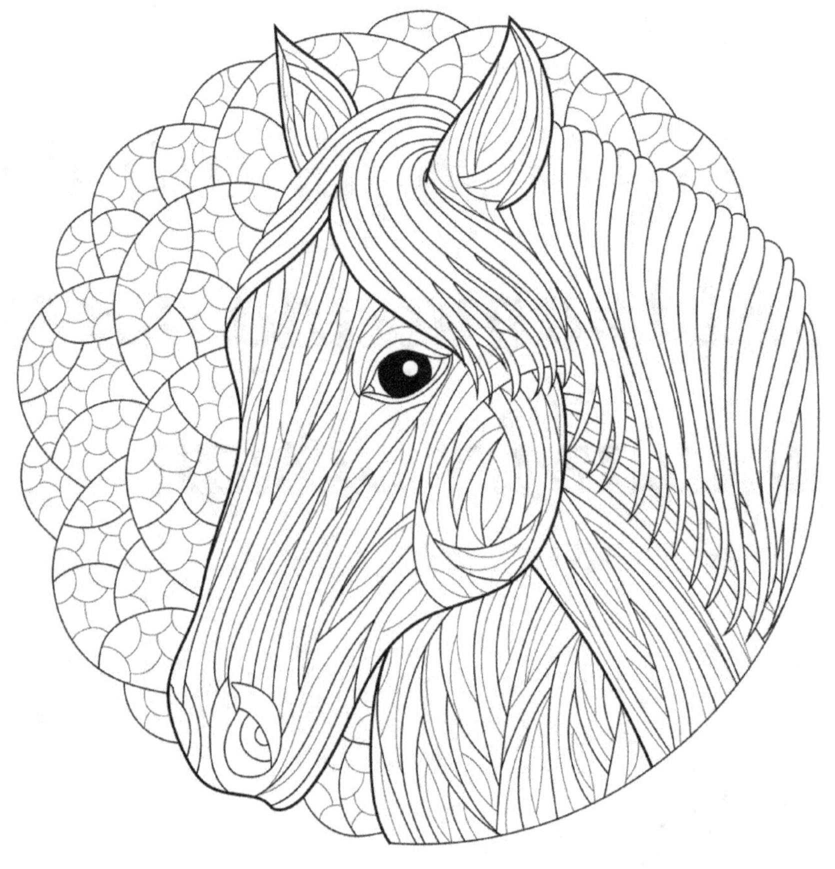

This book is belongs to

____

____

____

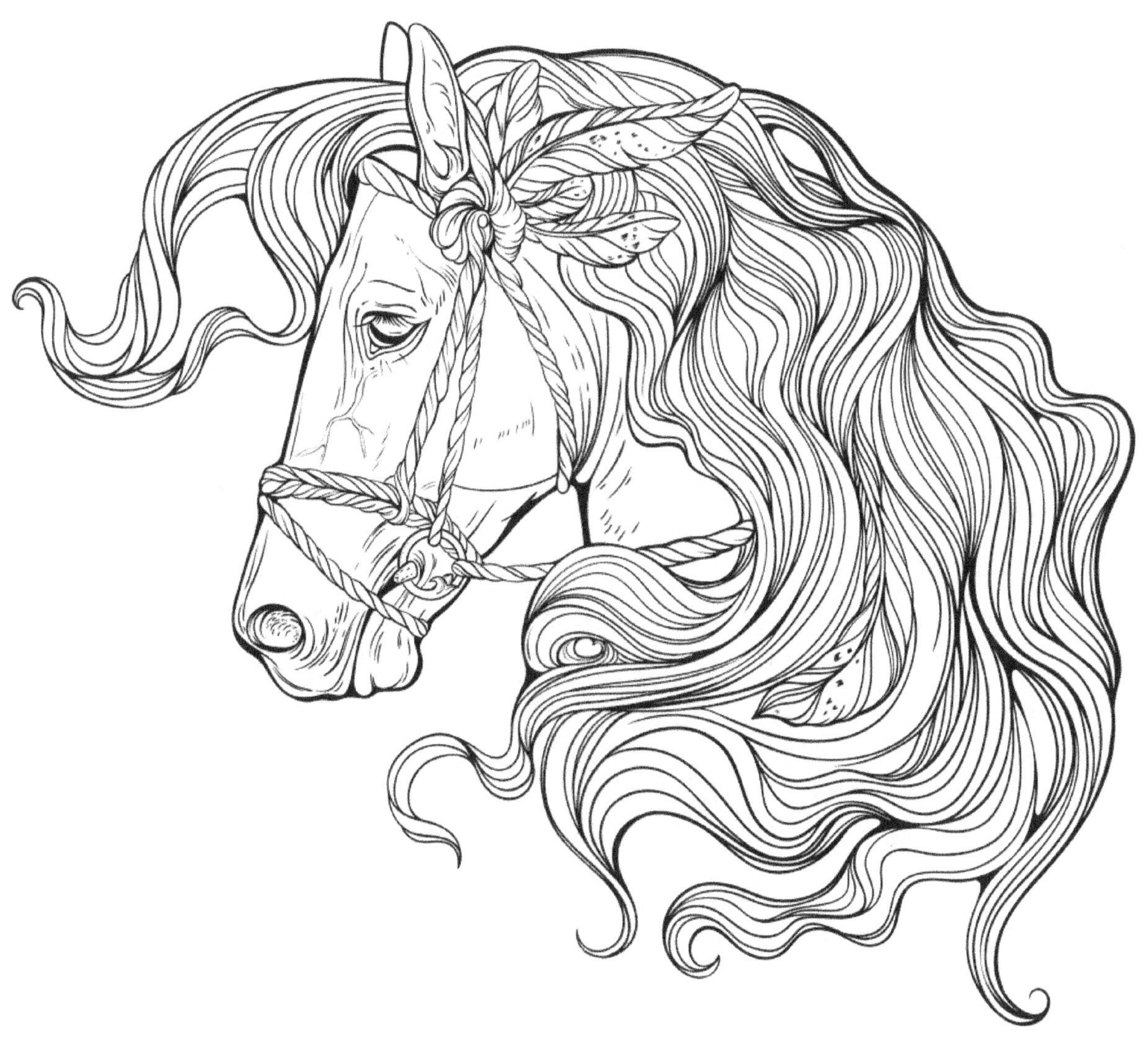

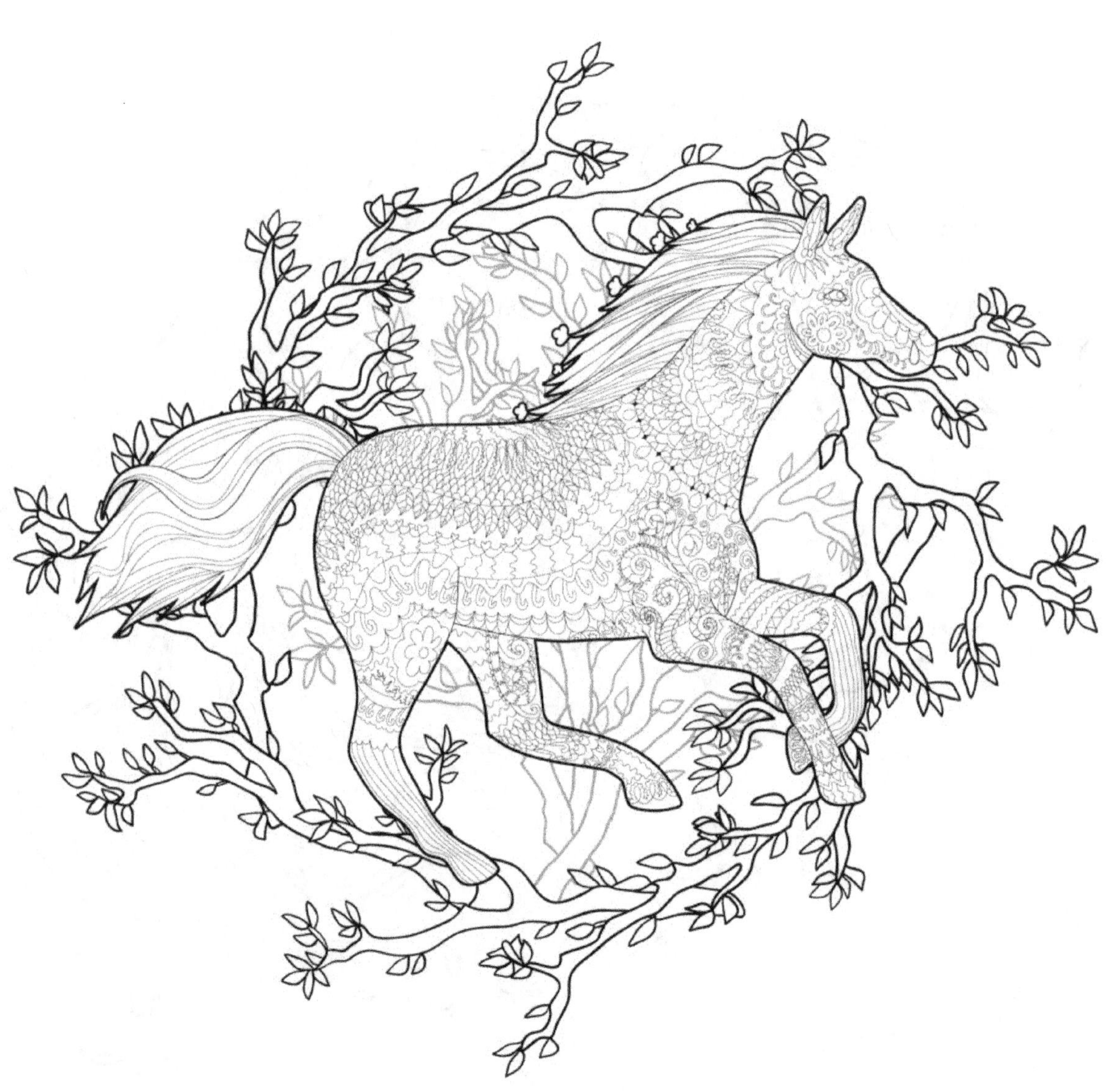

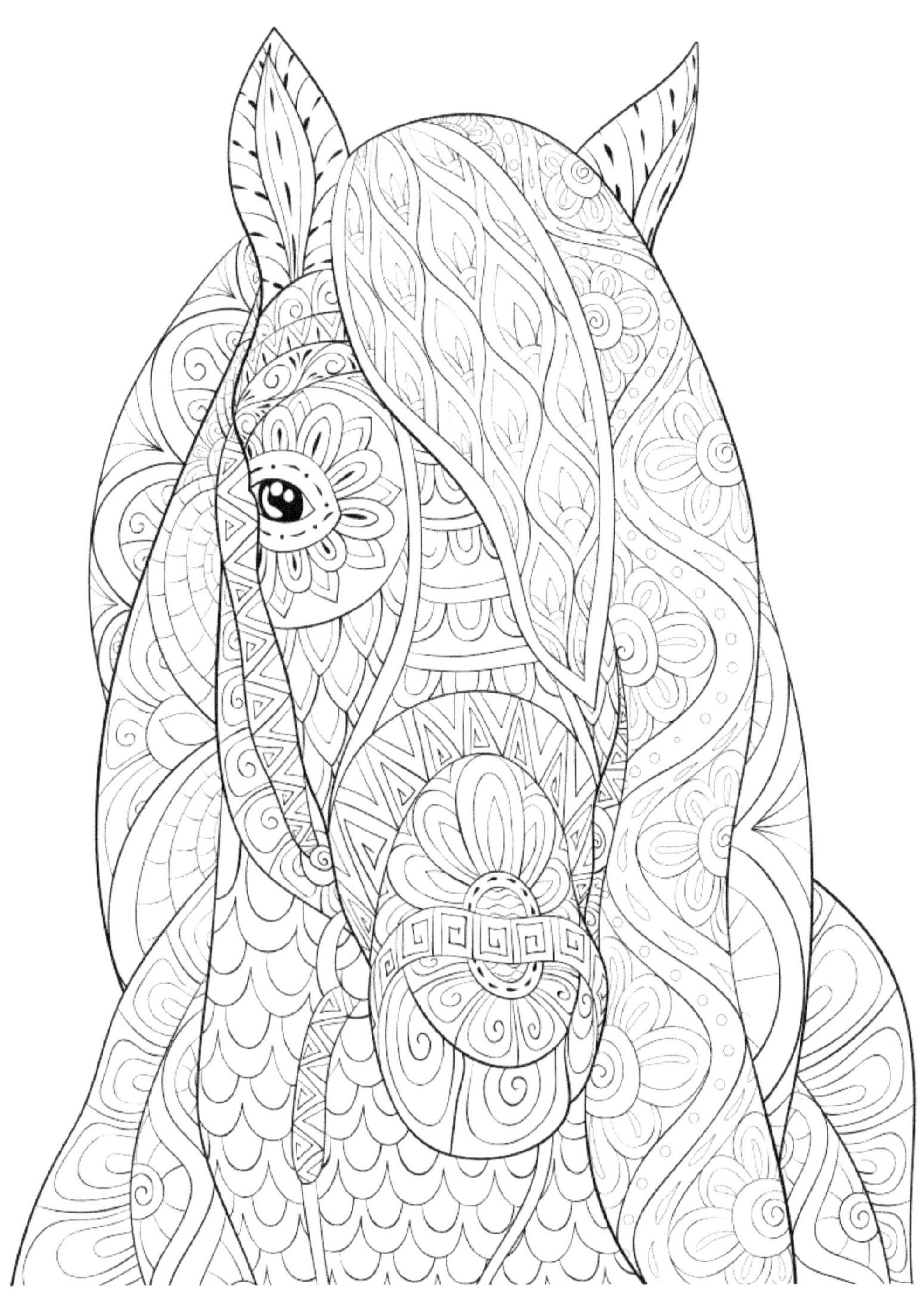

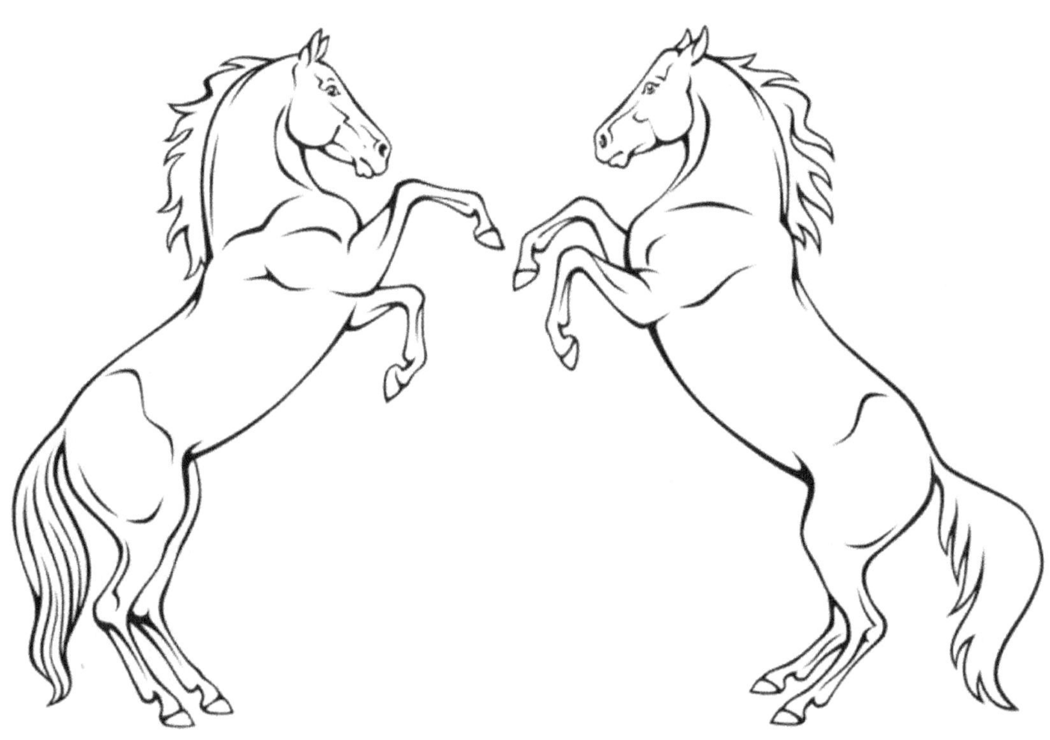

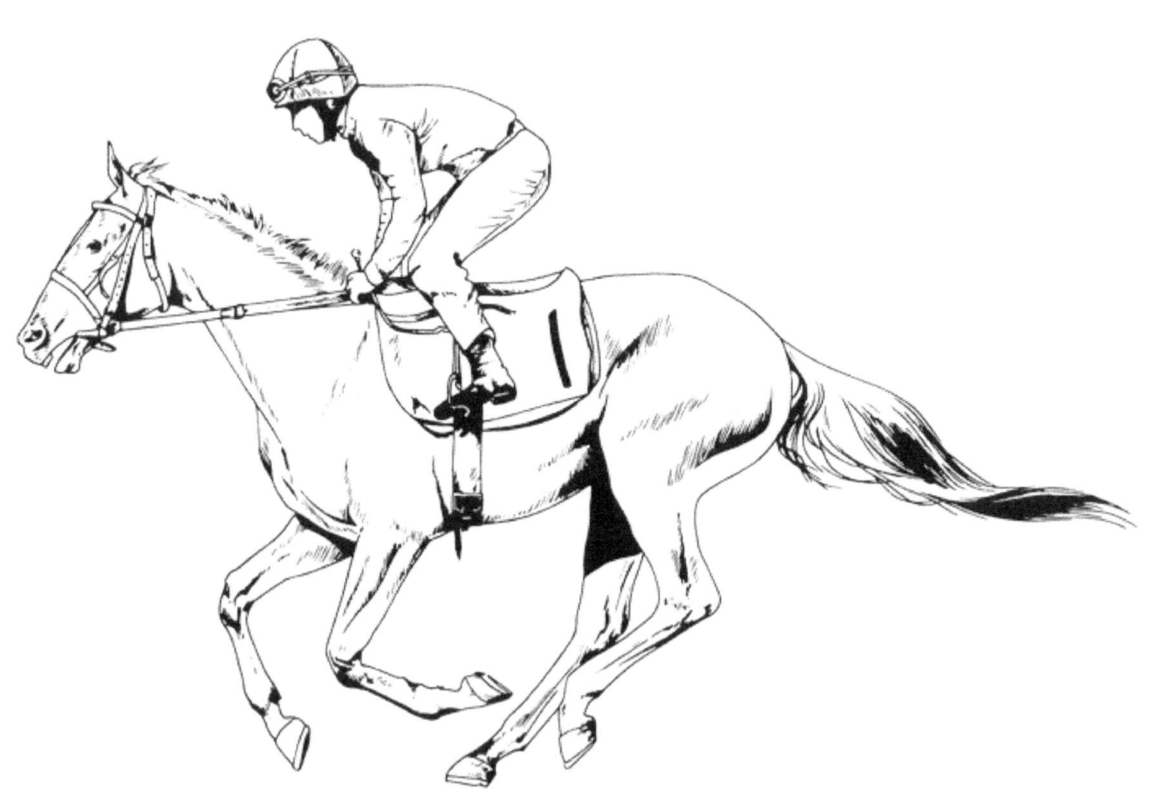

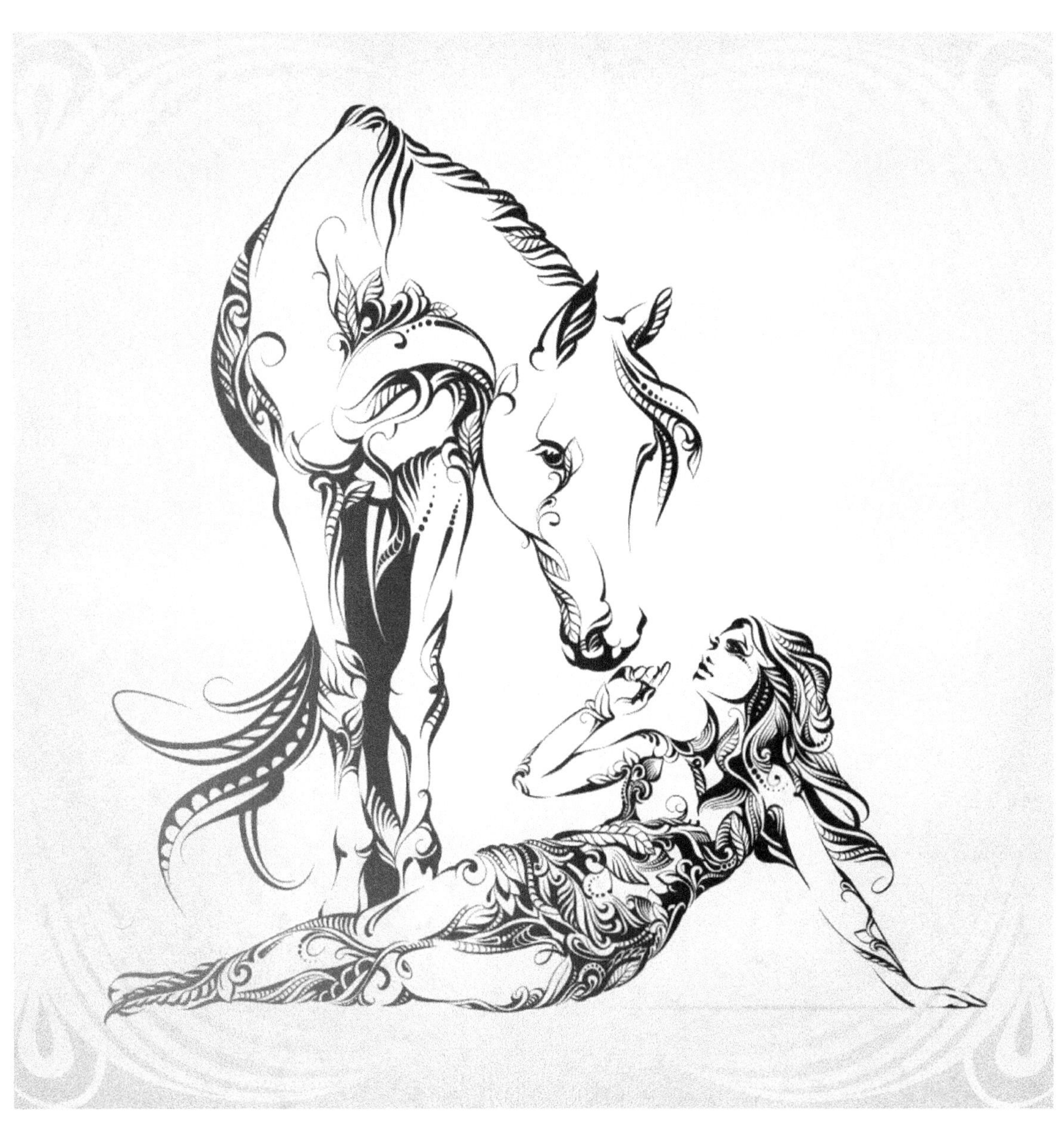

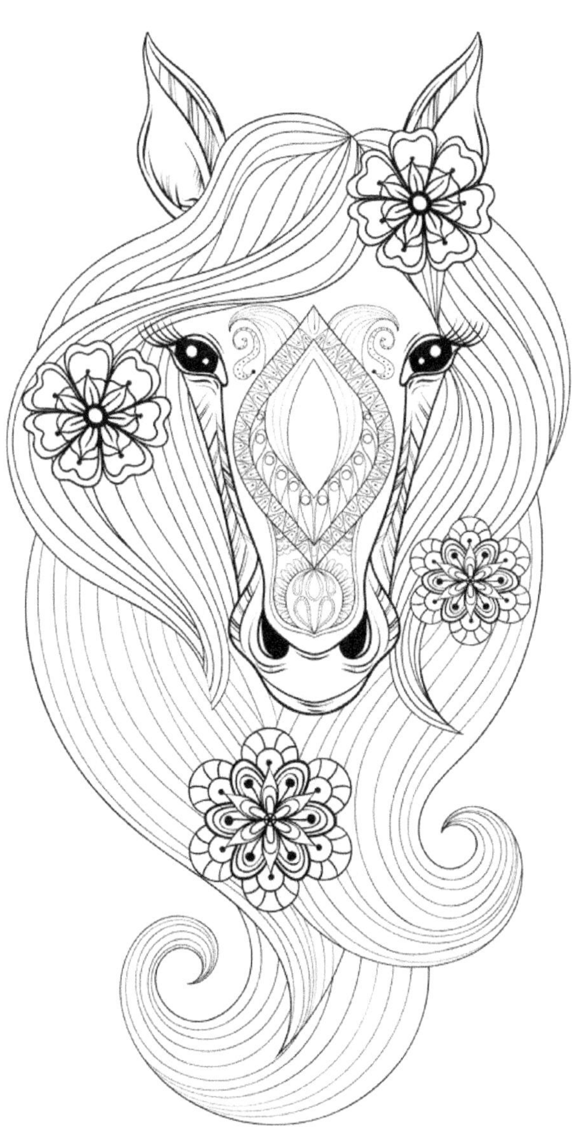

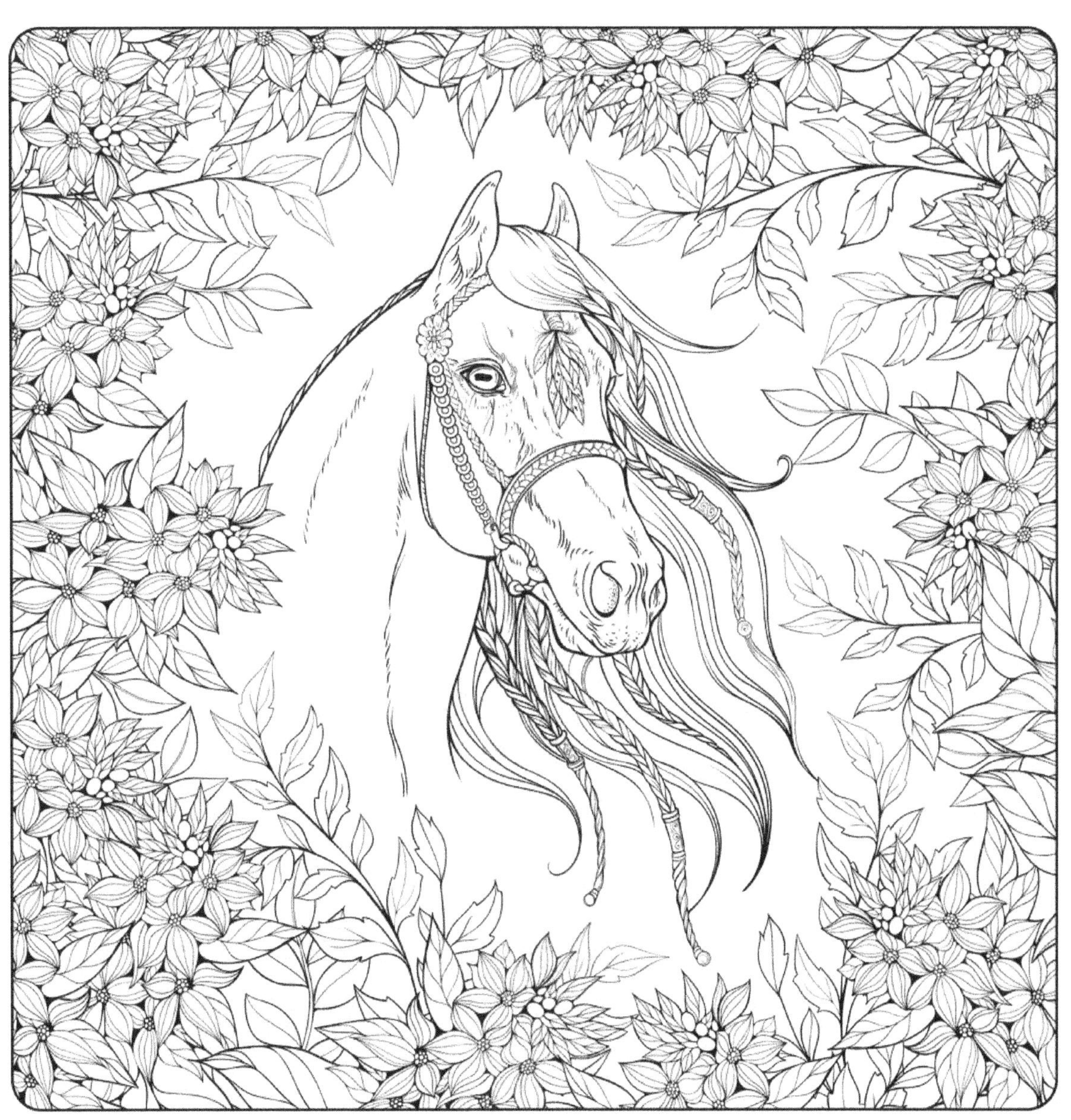

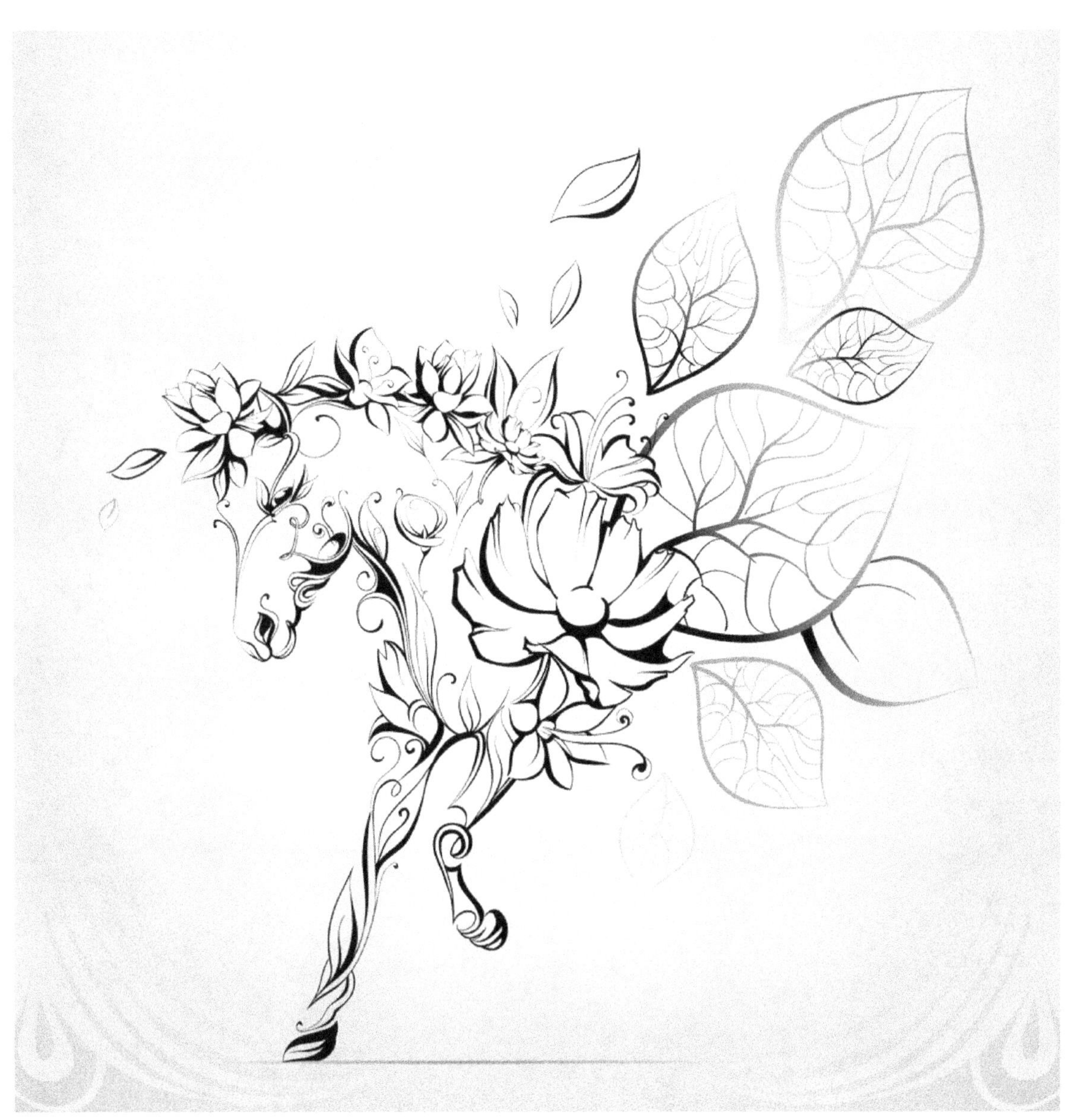

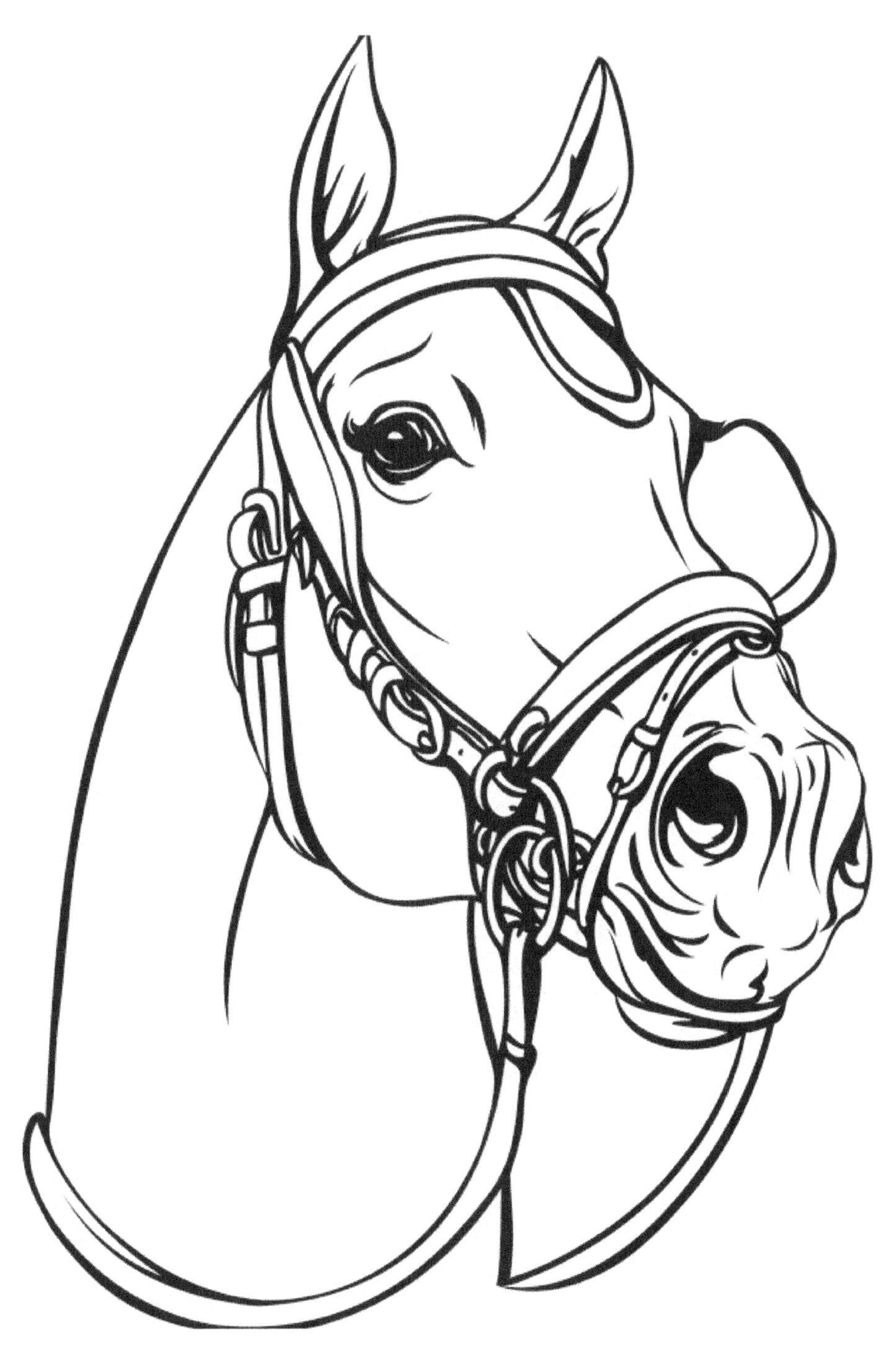

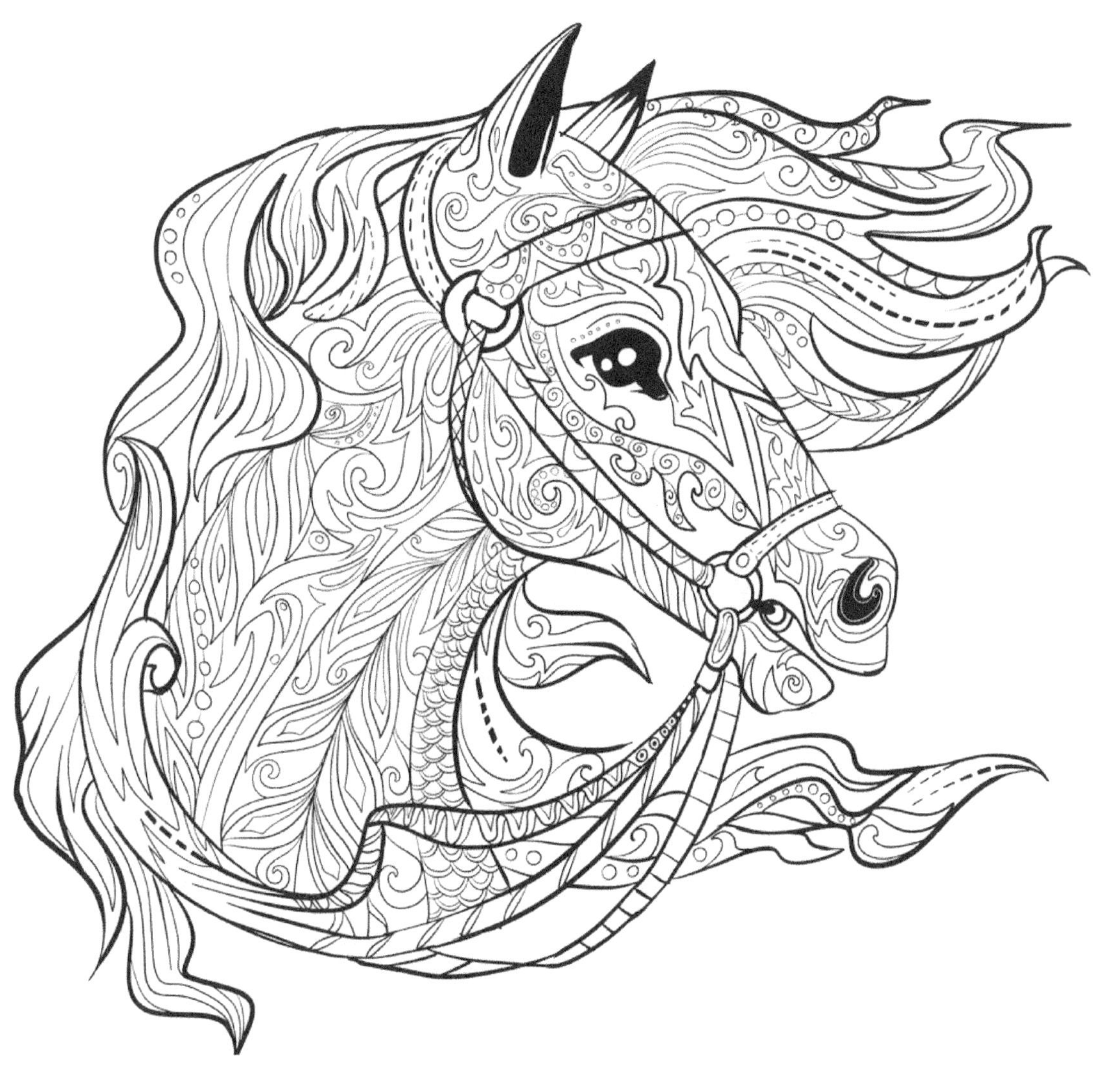

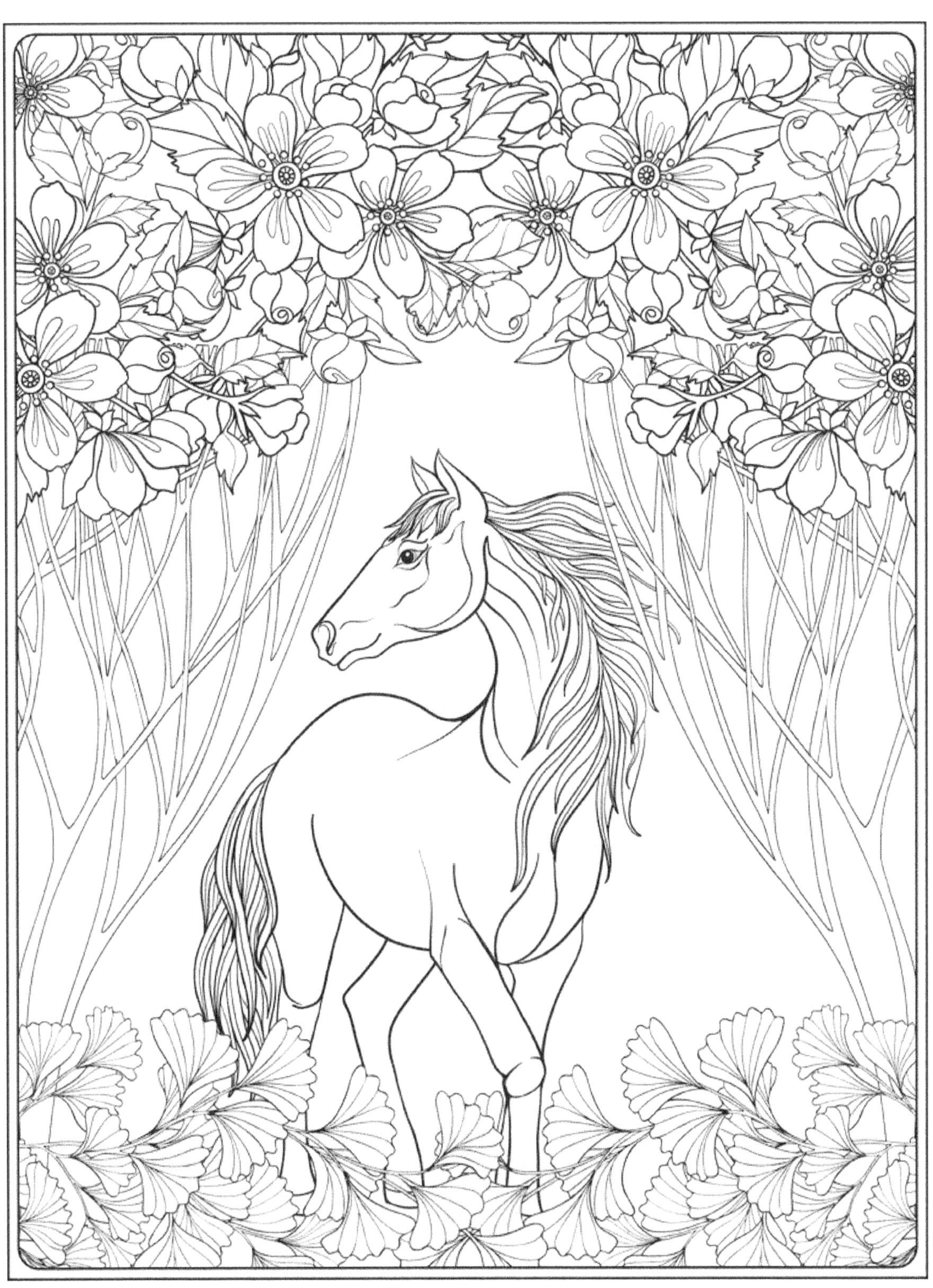

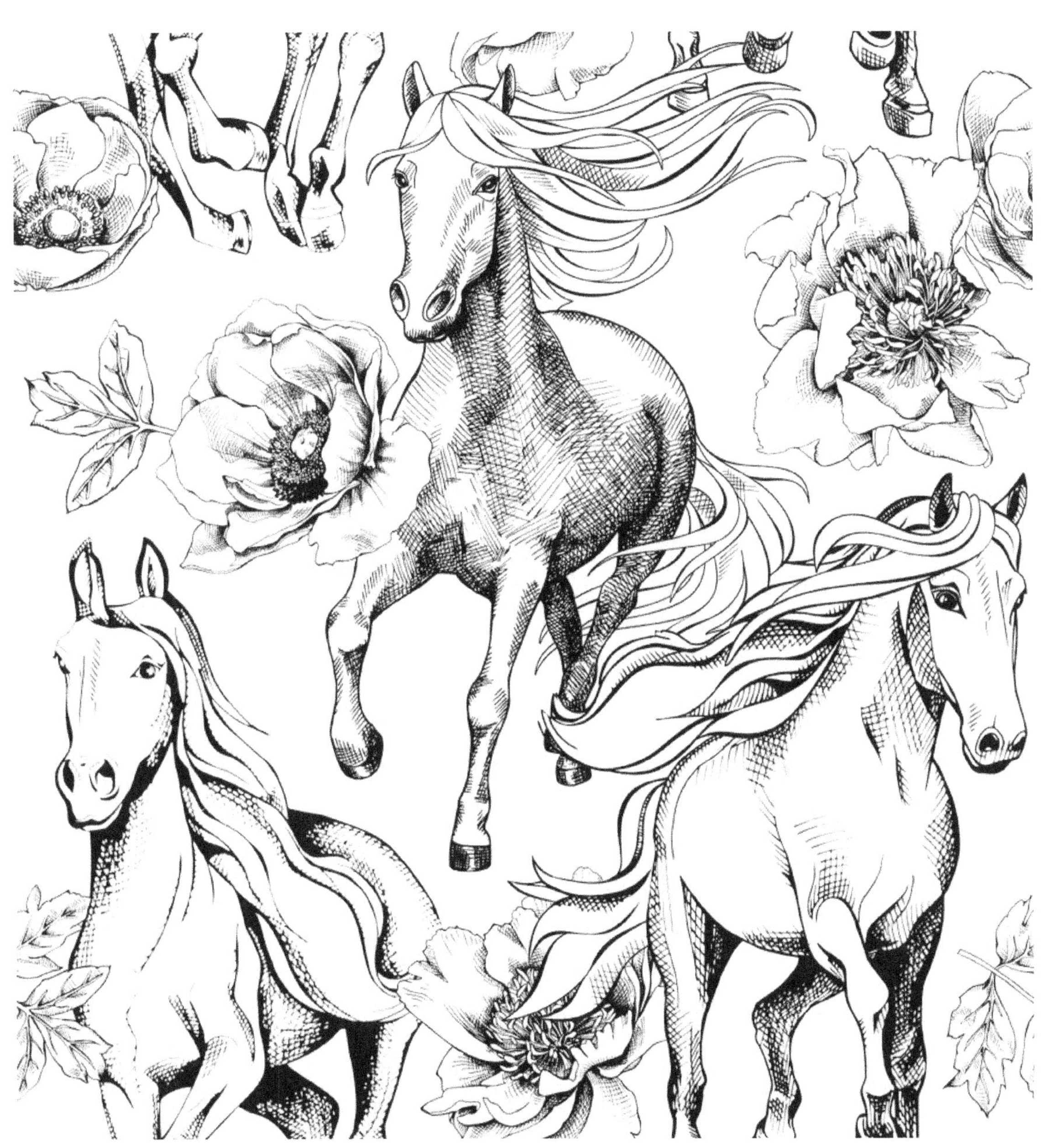

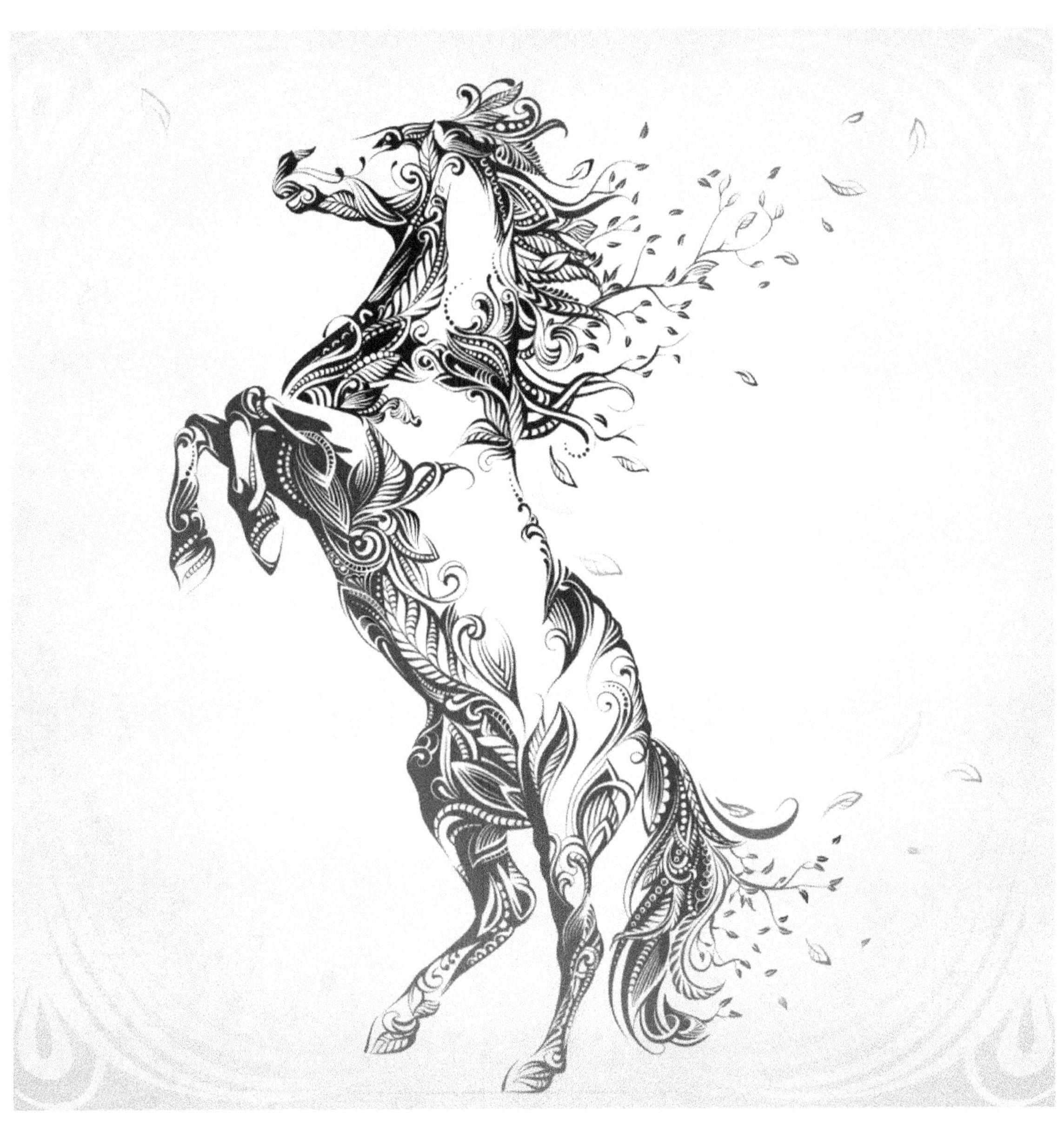

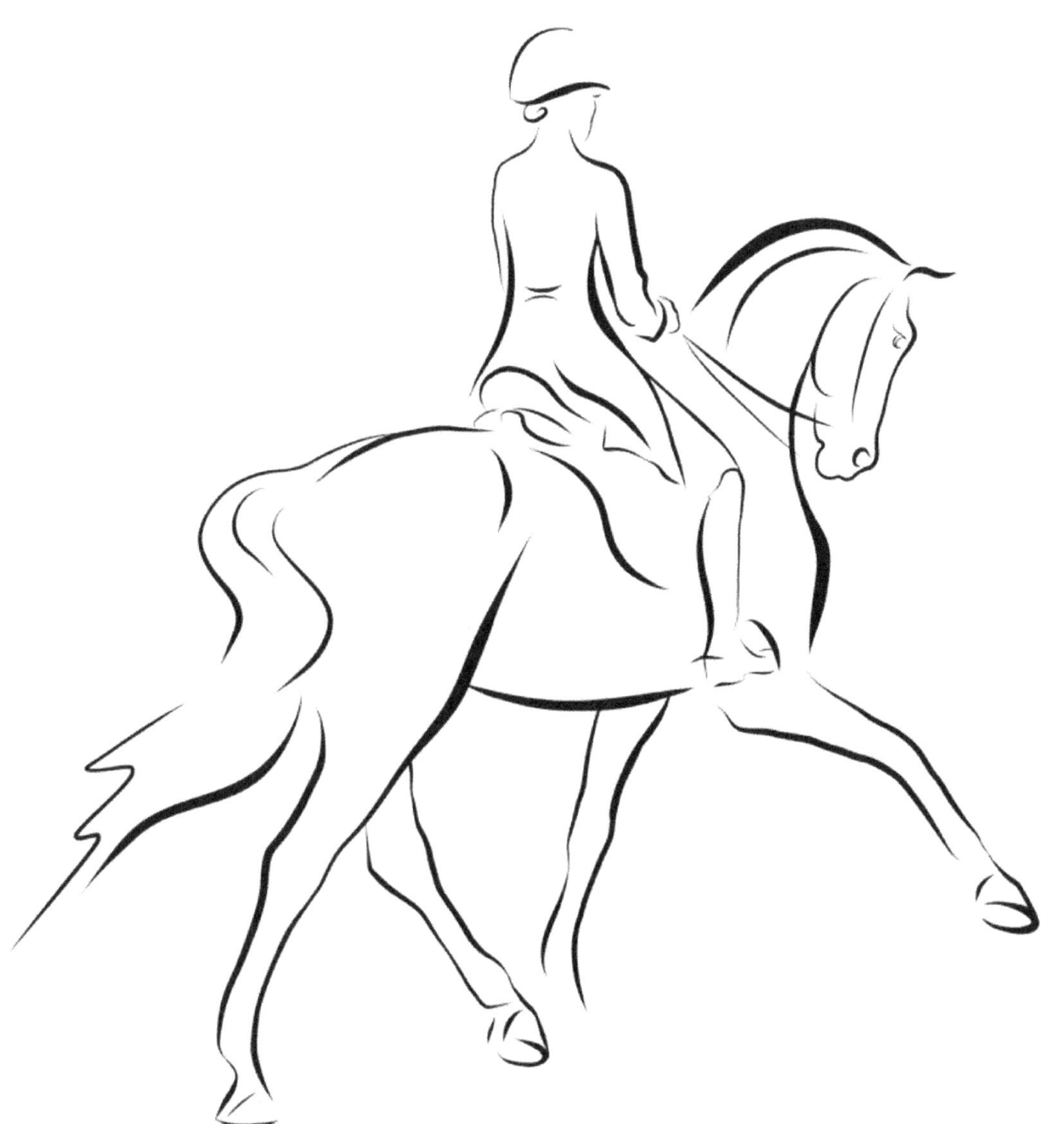

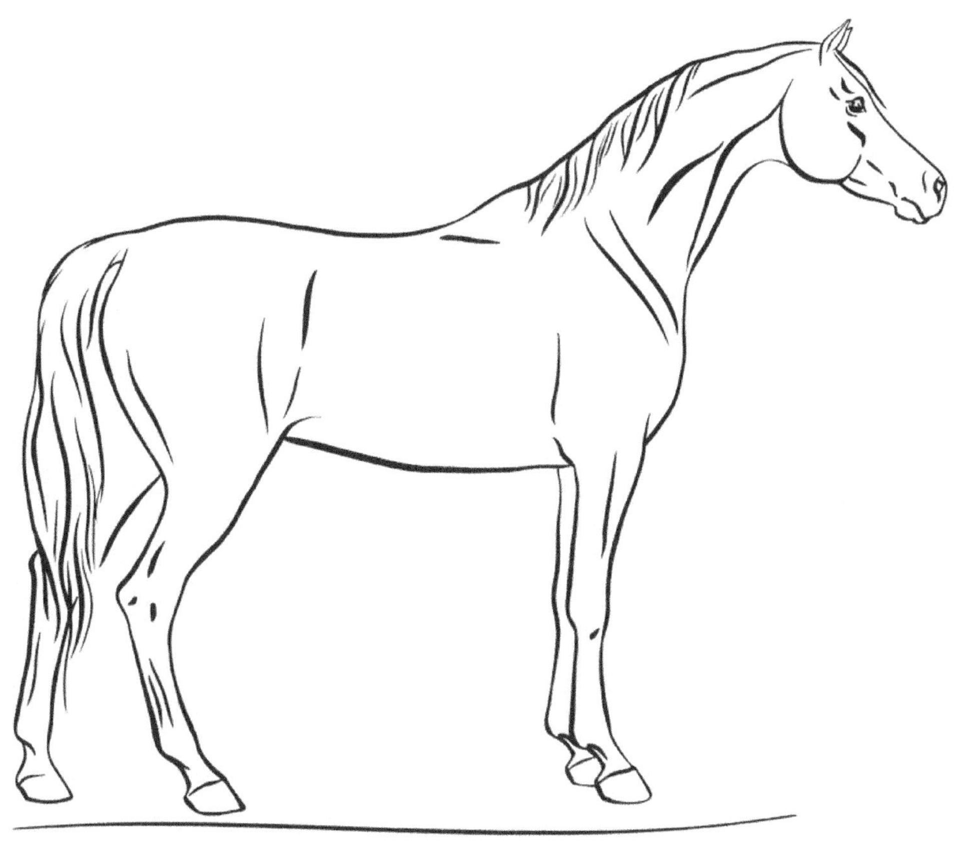

VECTOR | ALL
HEALTHY LIFE | SPORT

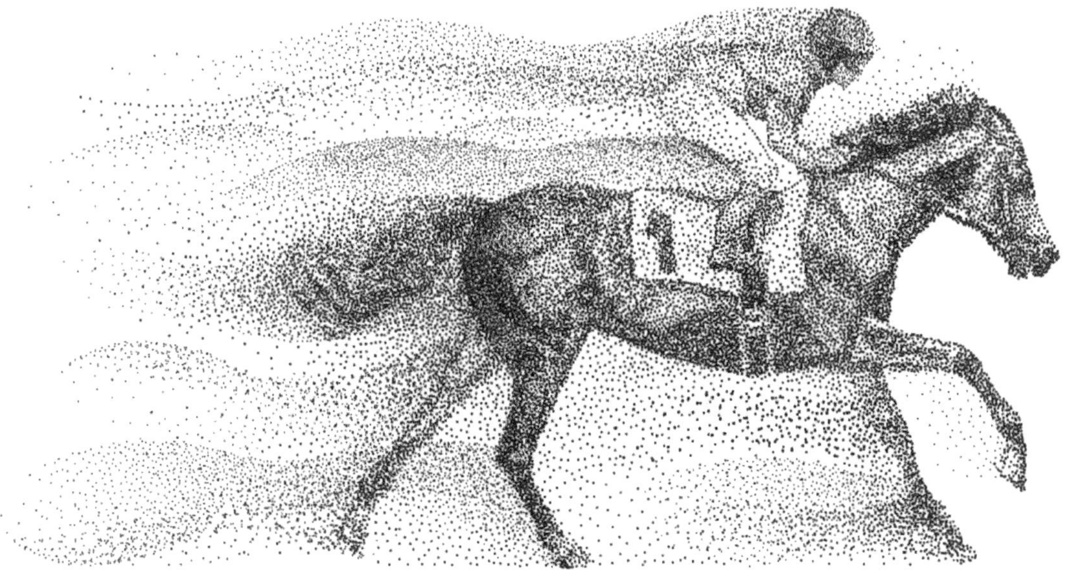

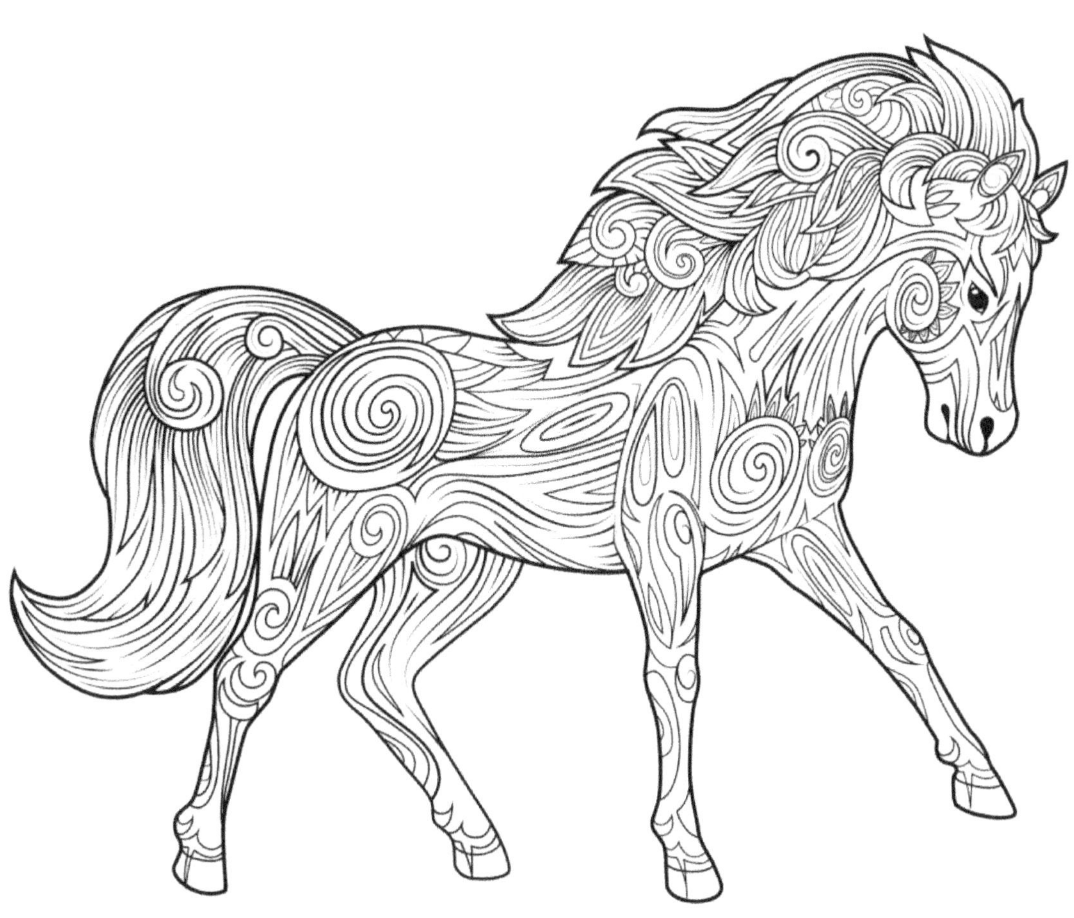

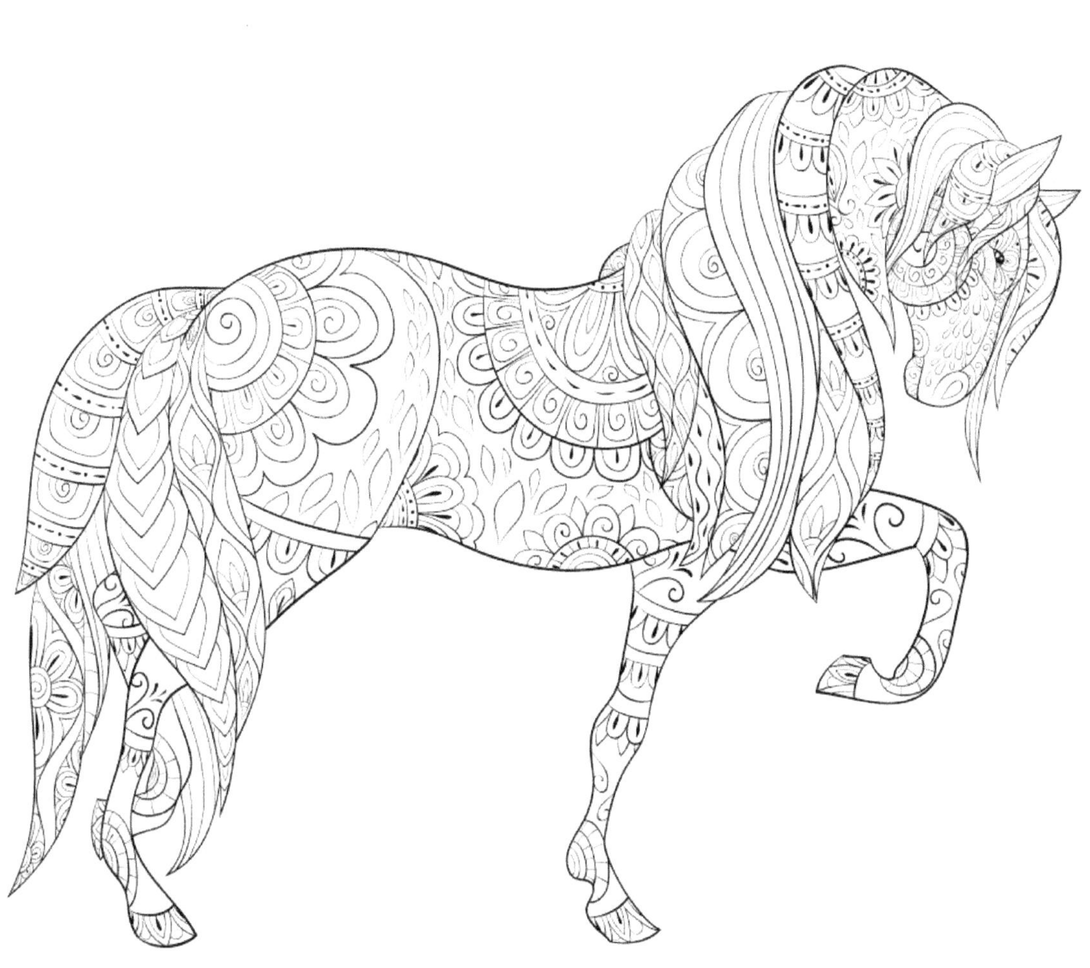

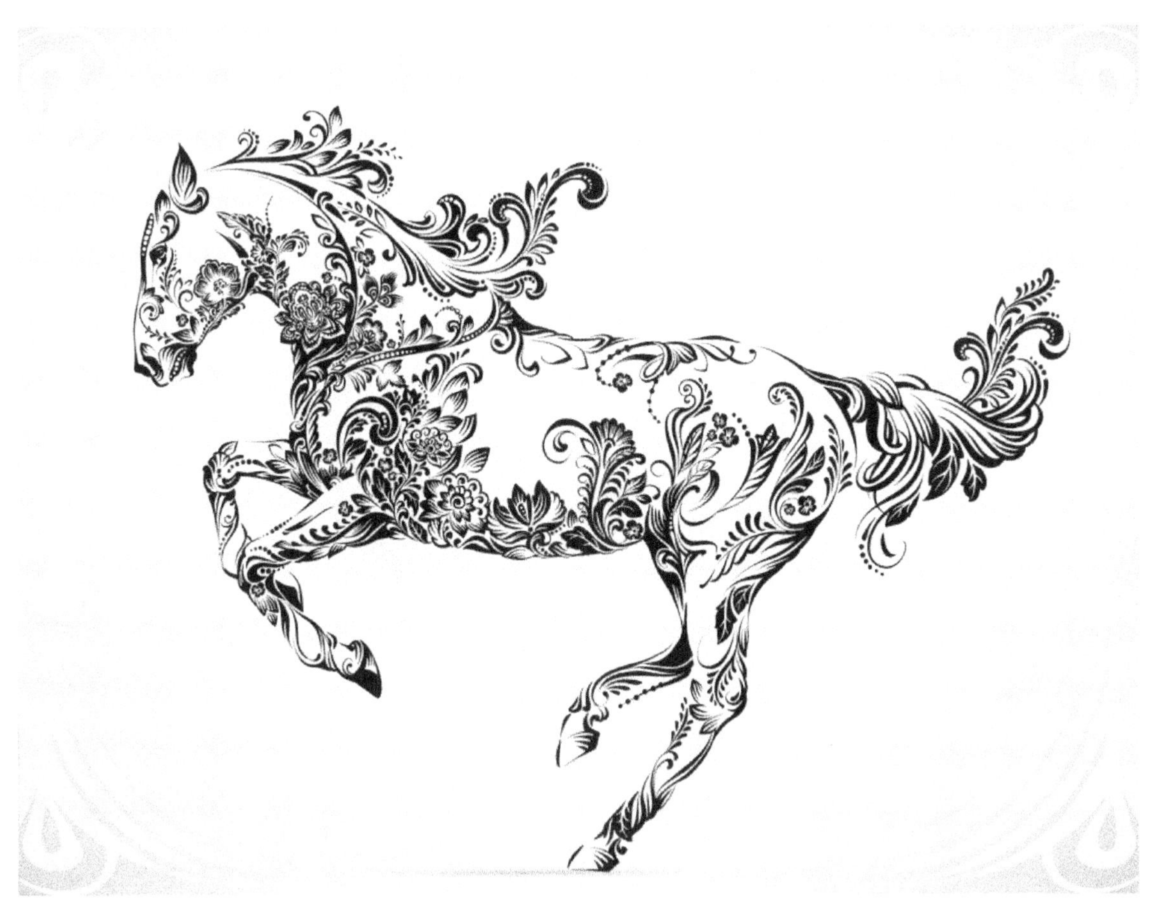

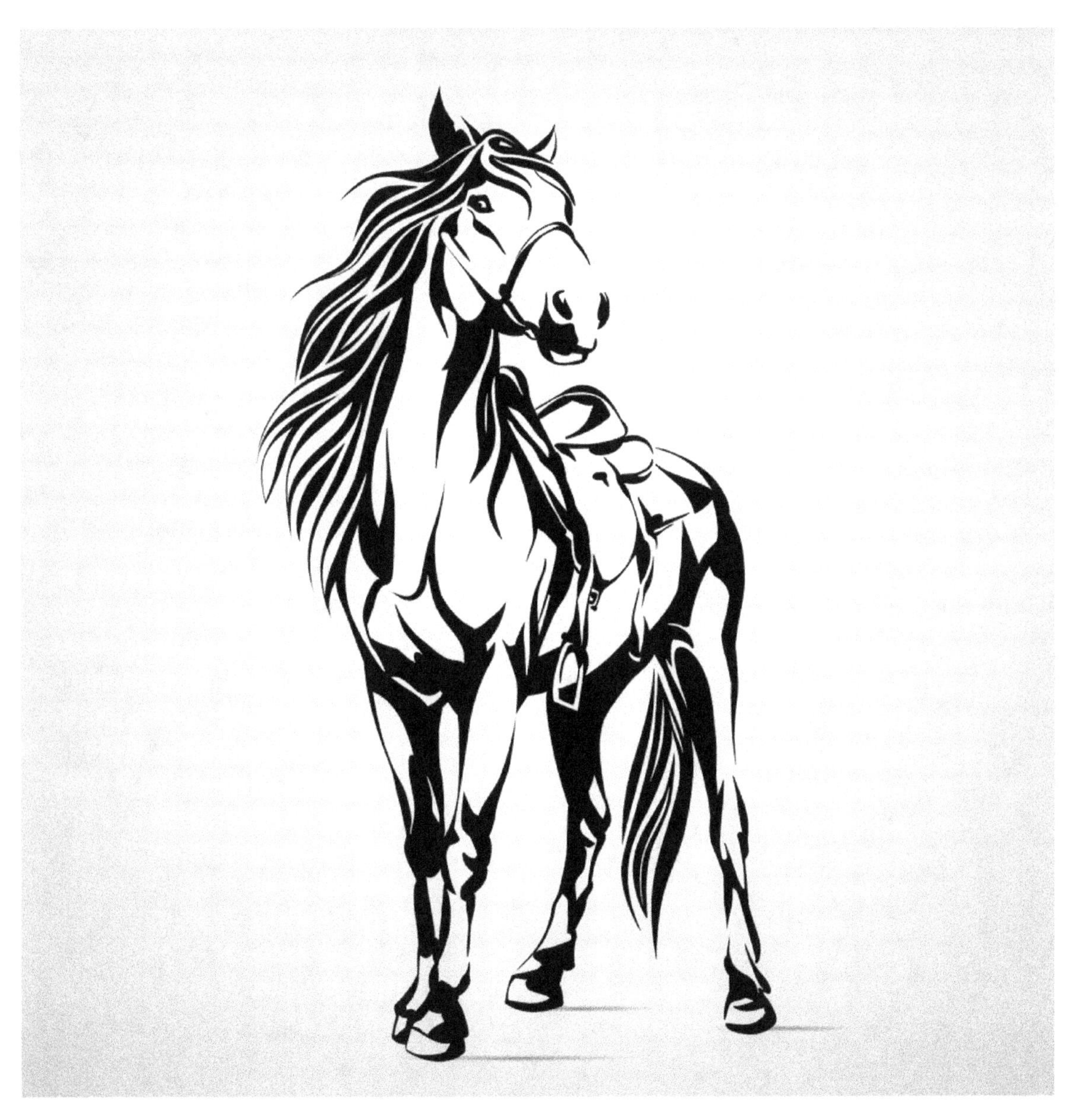

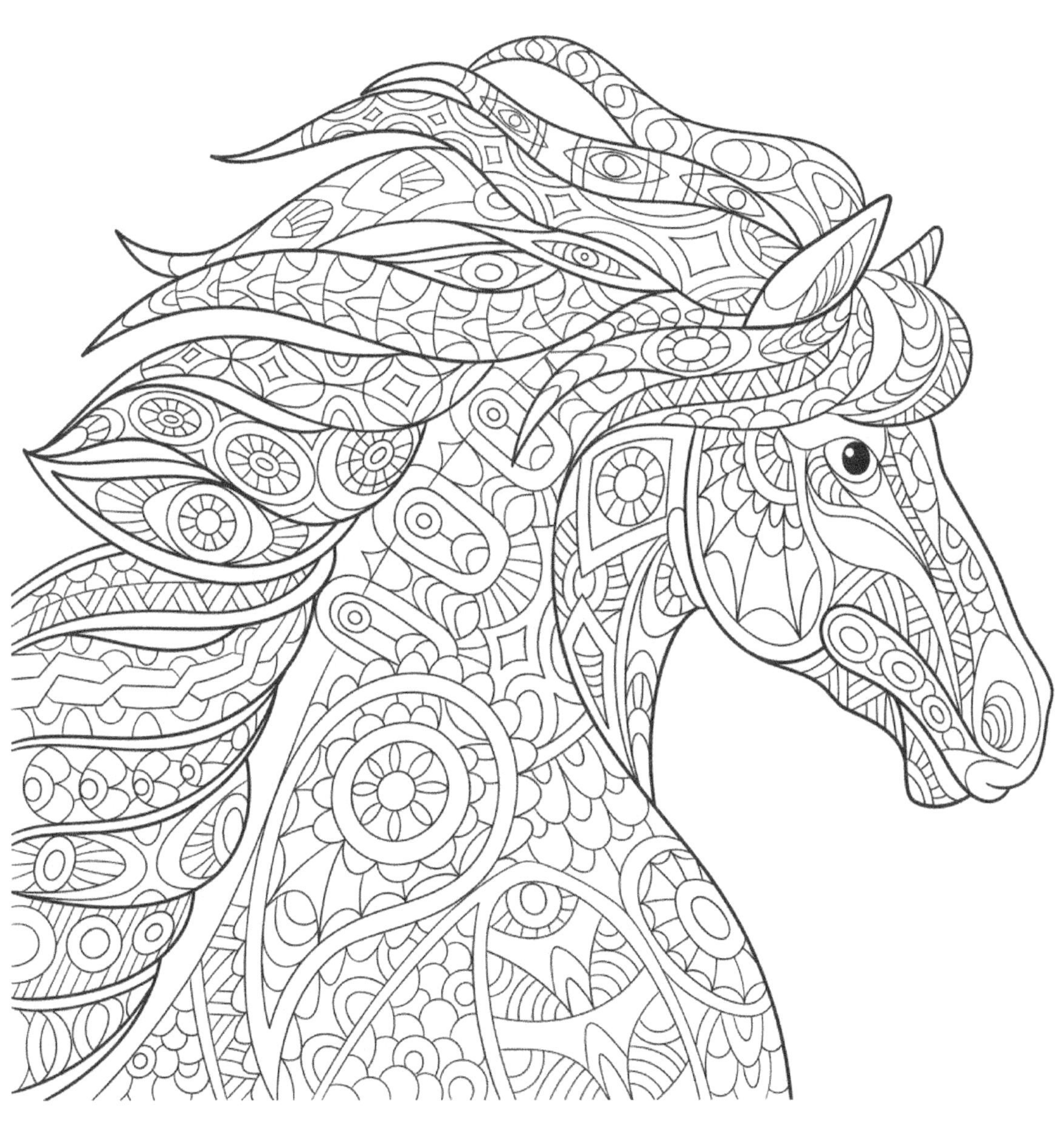

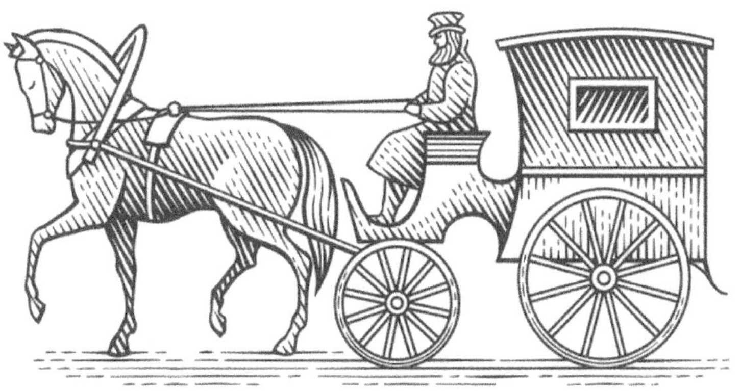

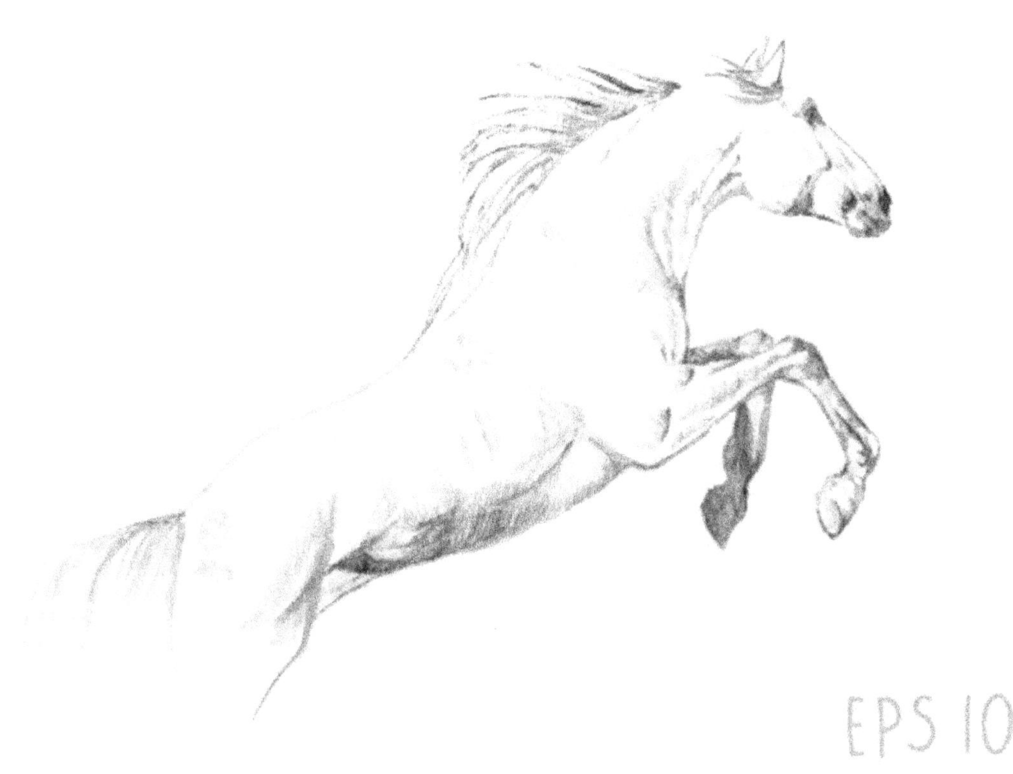
EPS 10

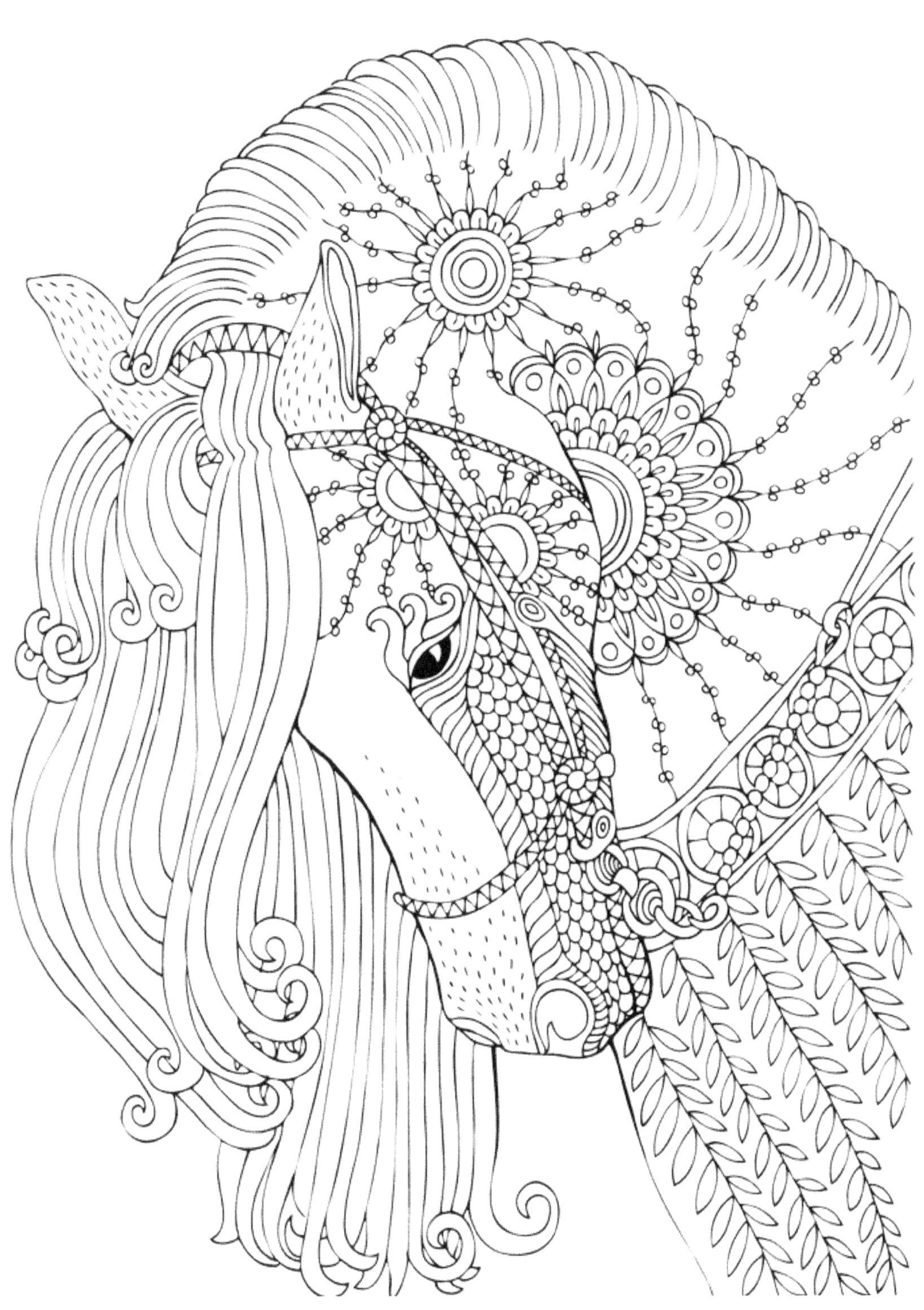

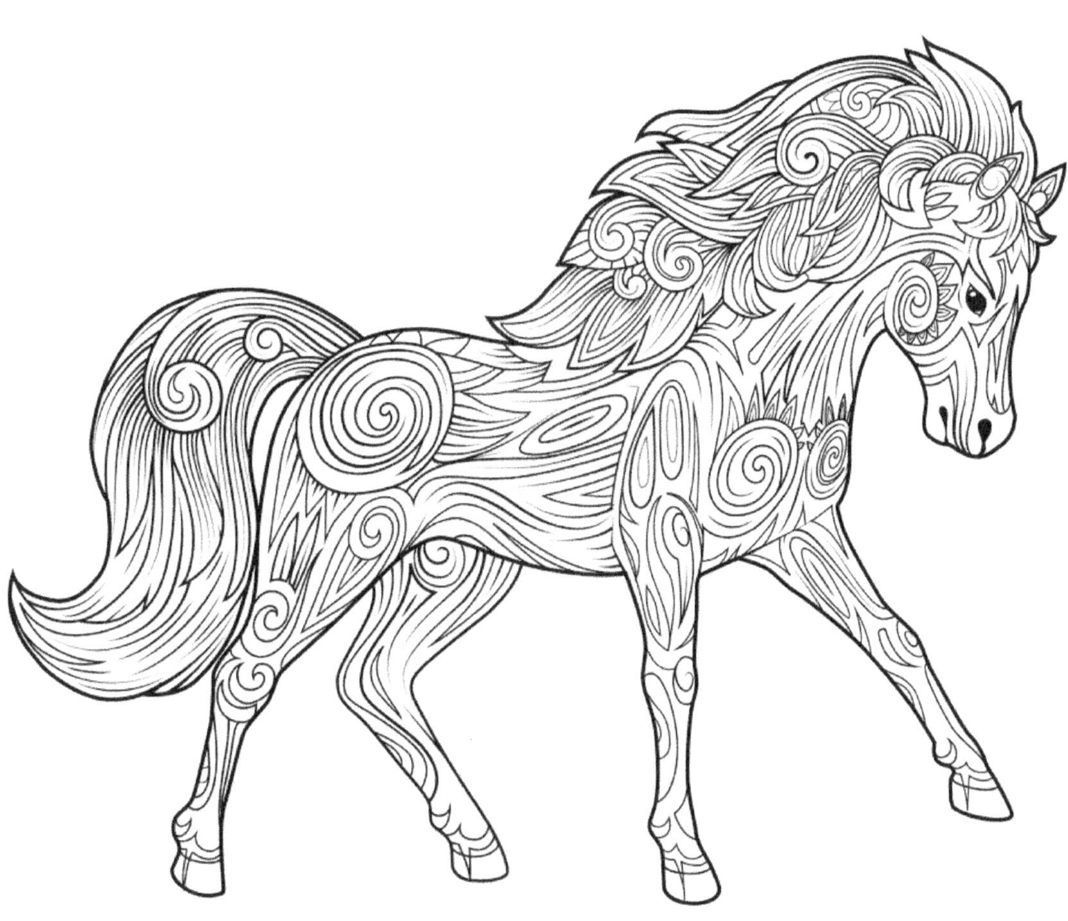

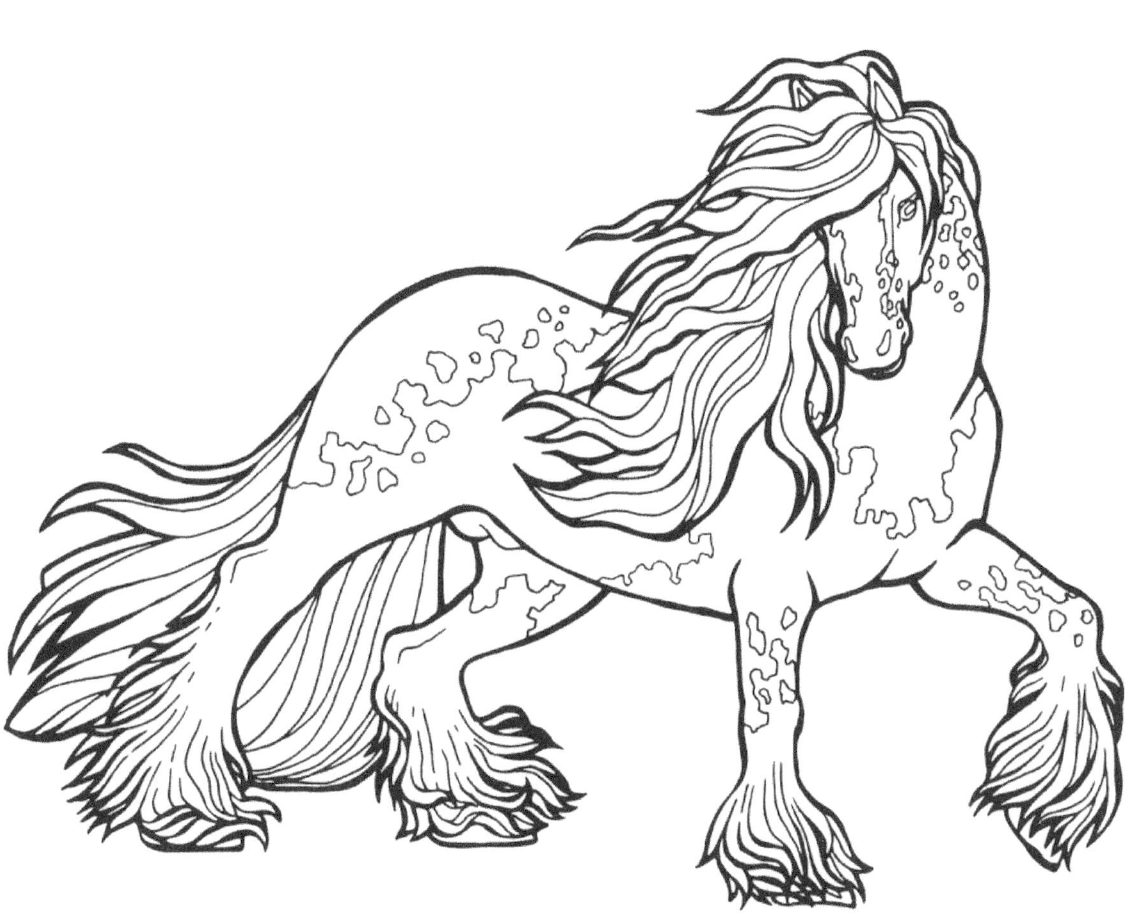

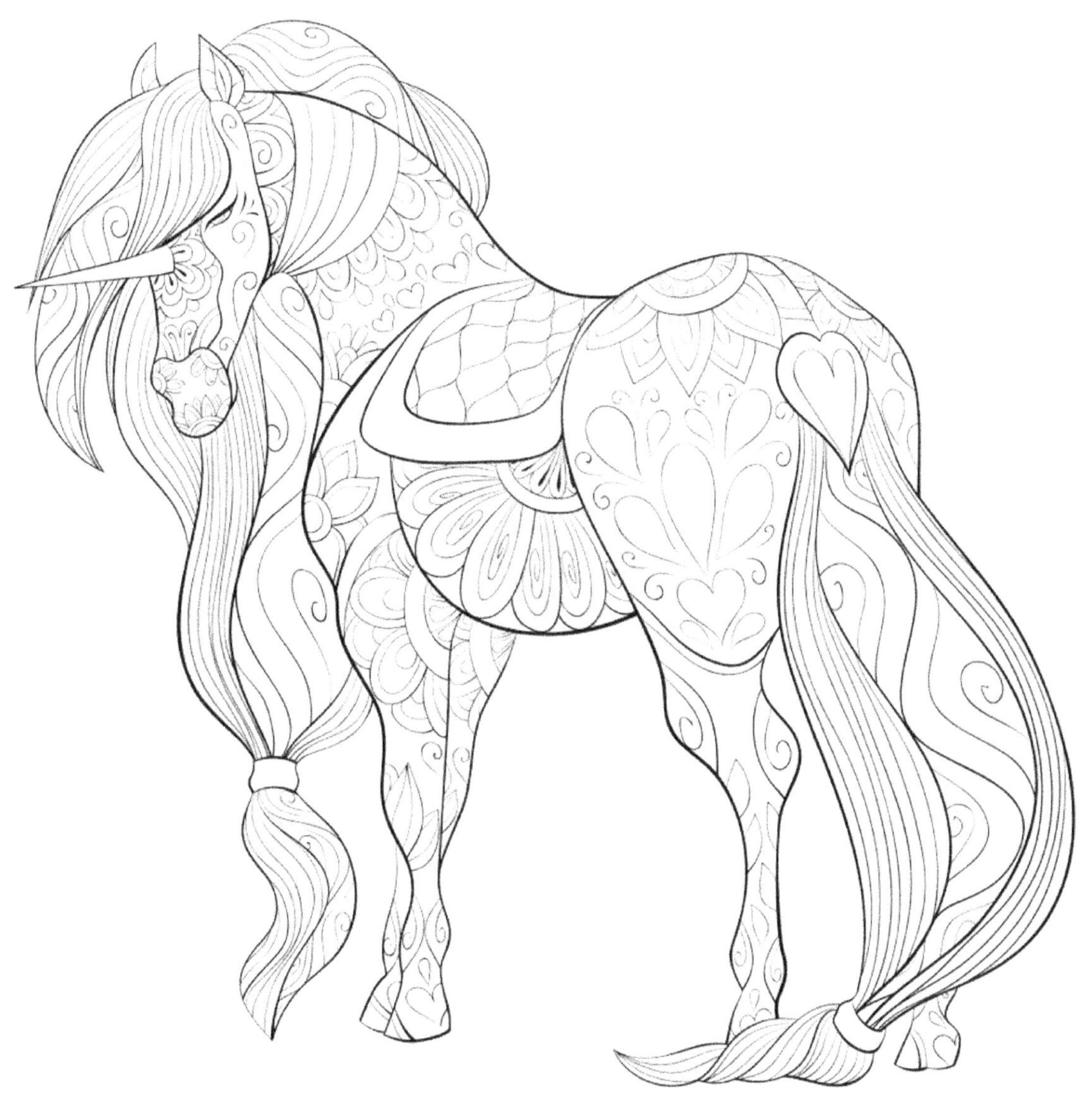

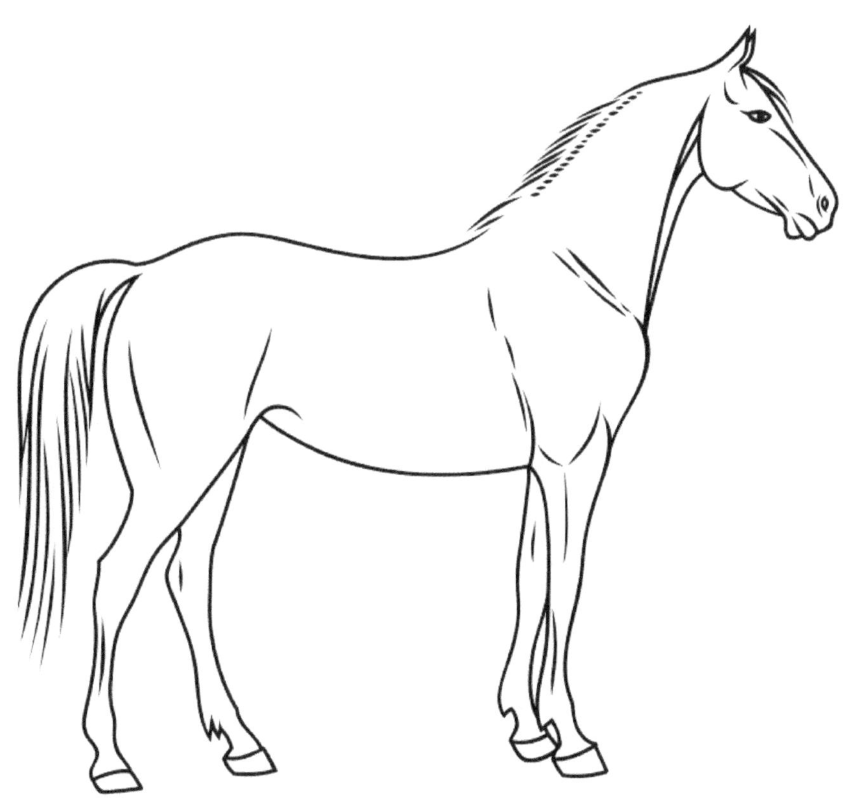

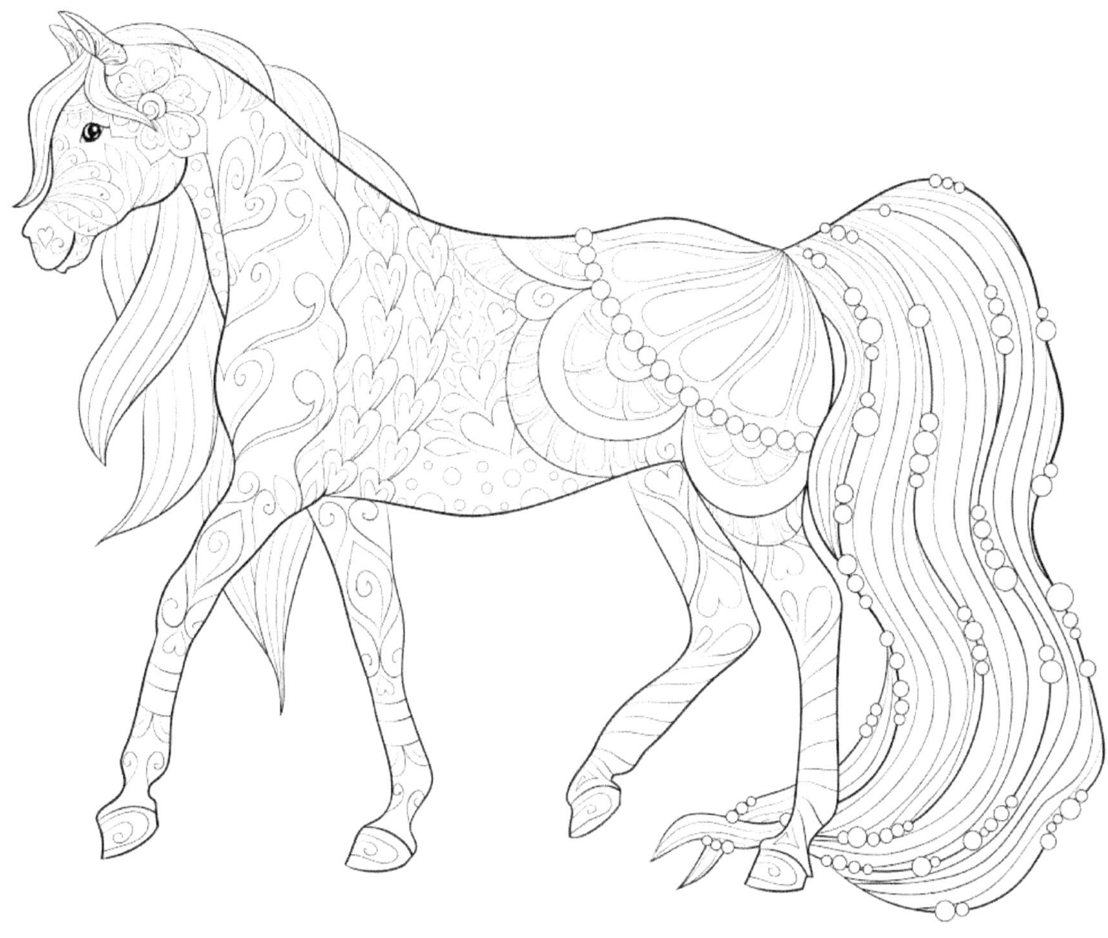

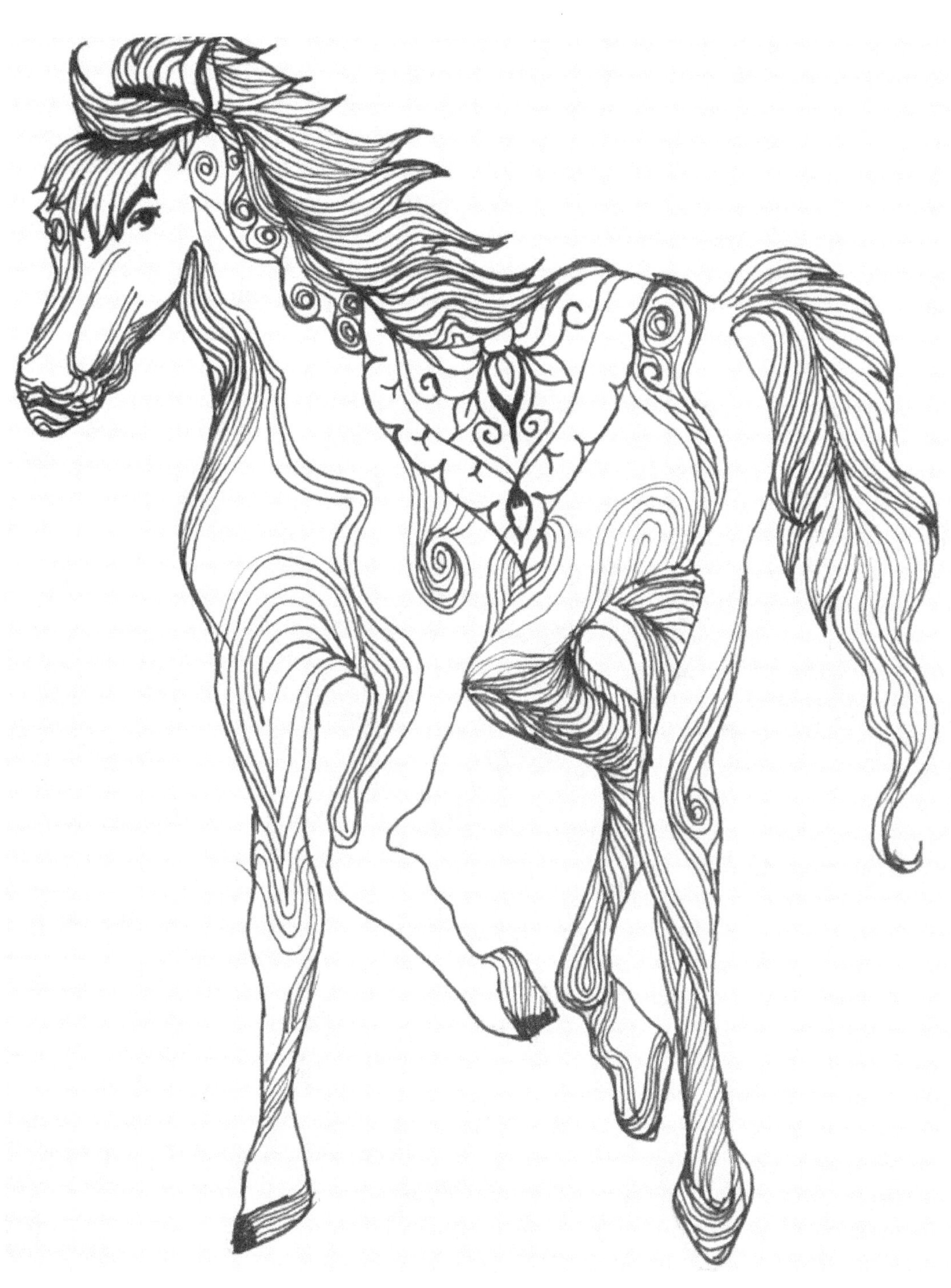

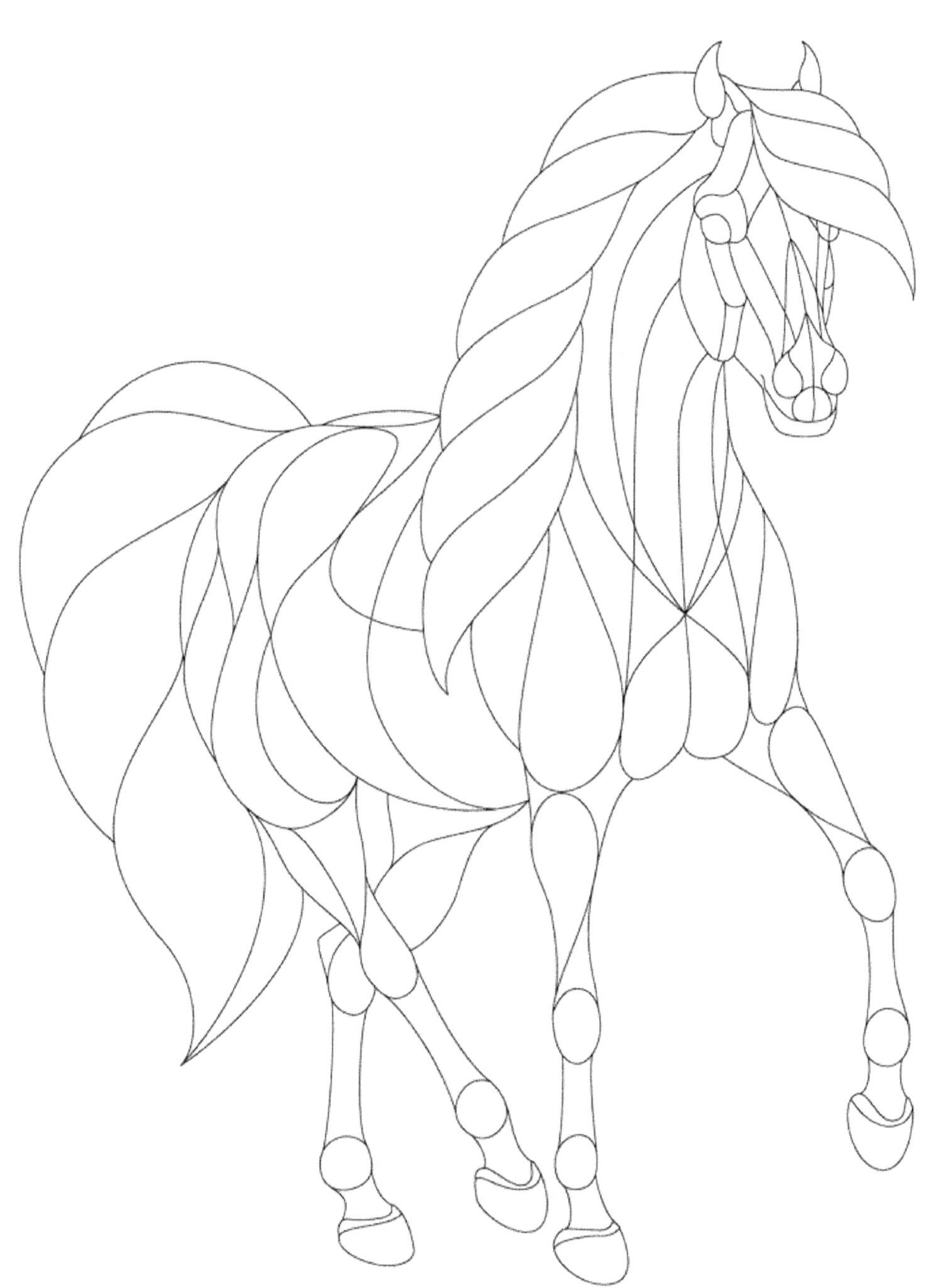

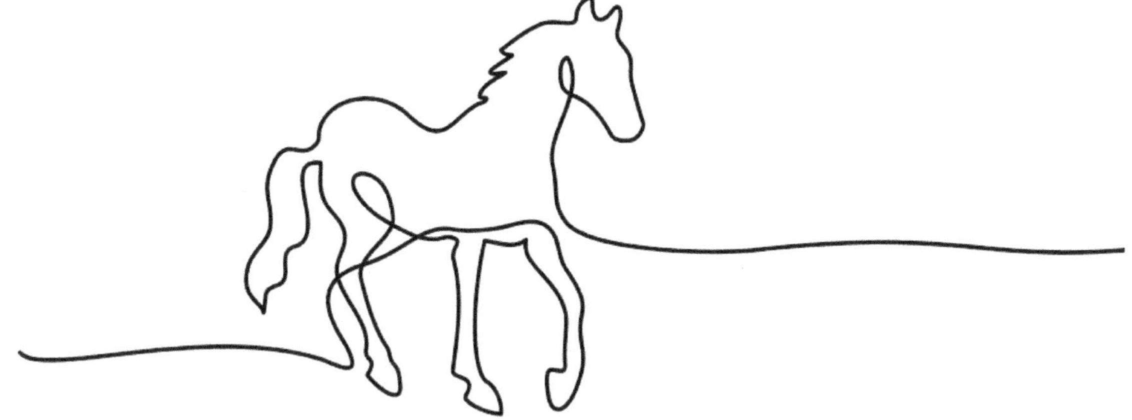

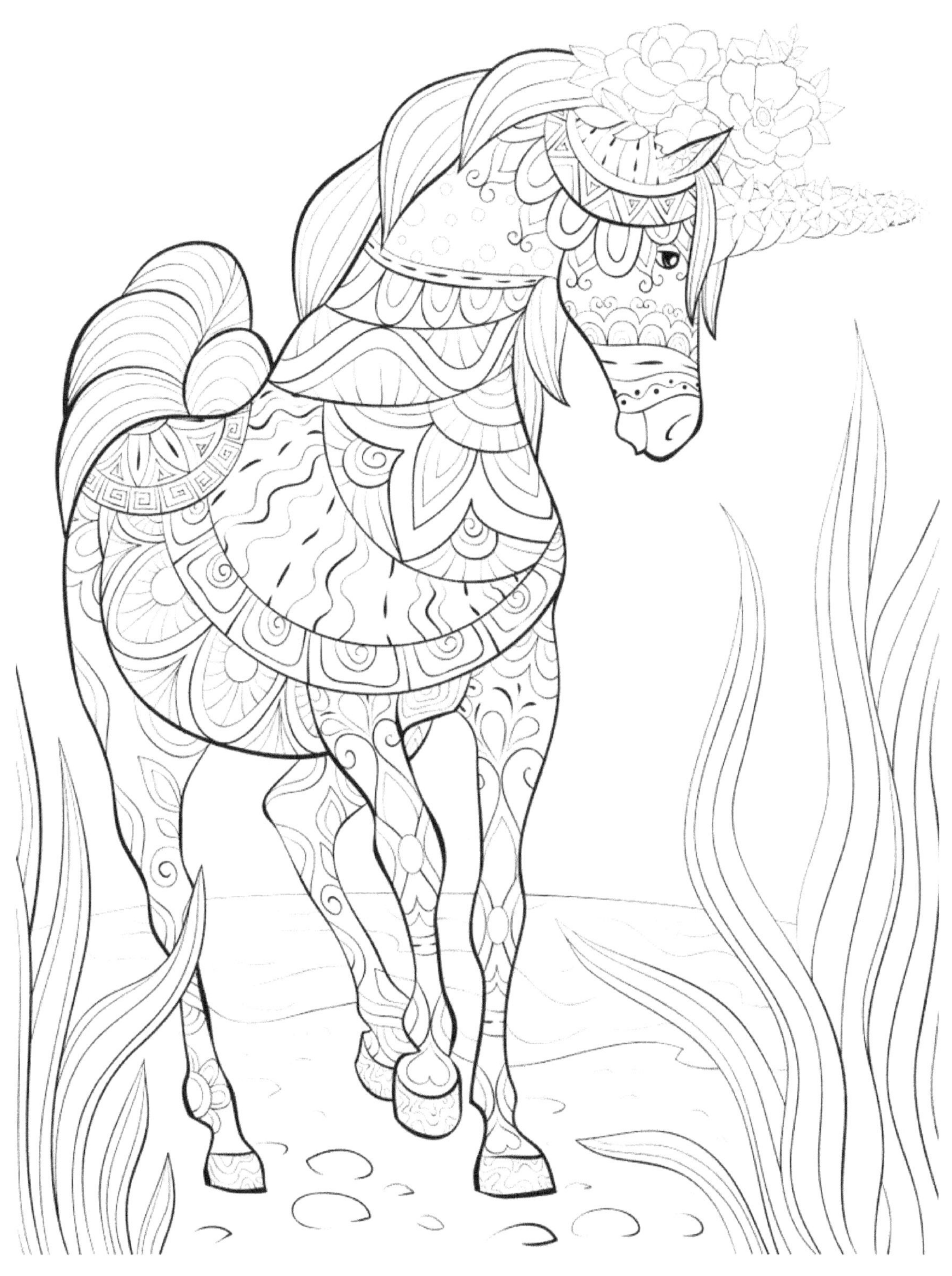

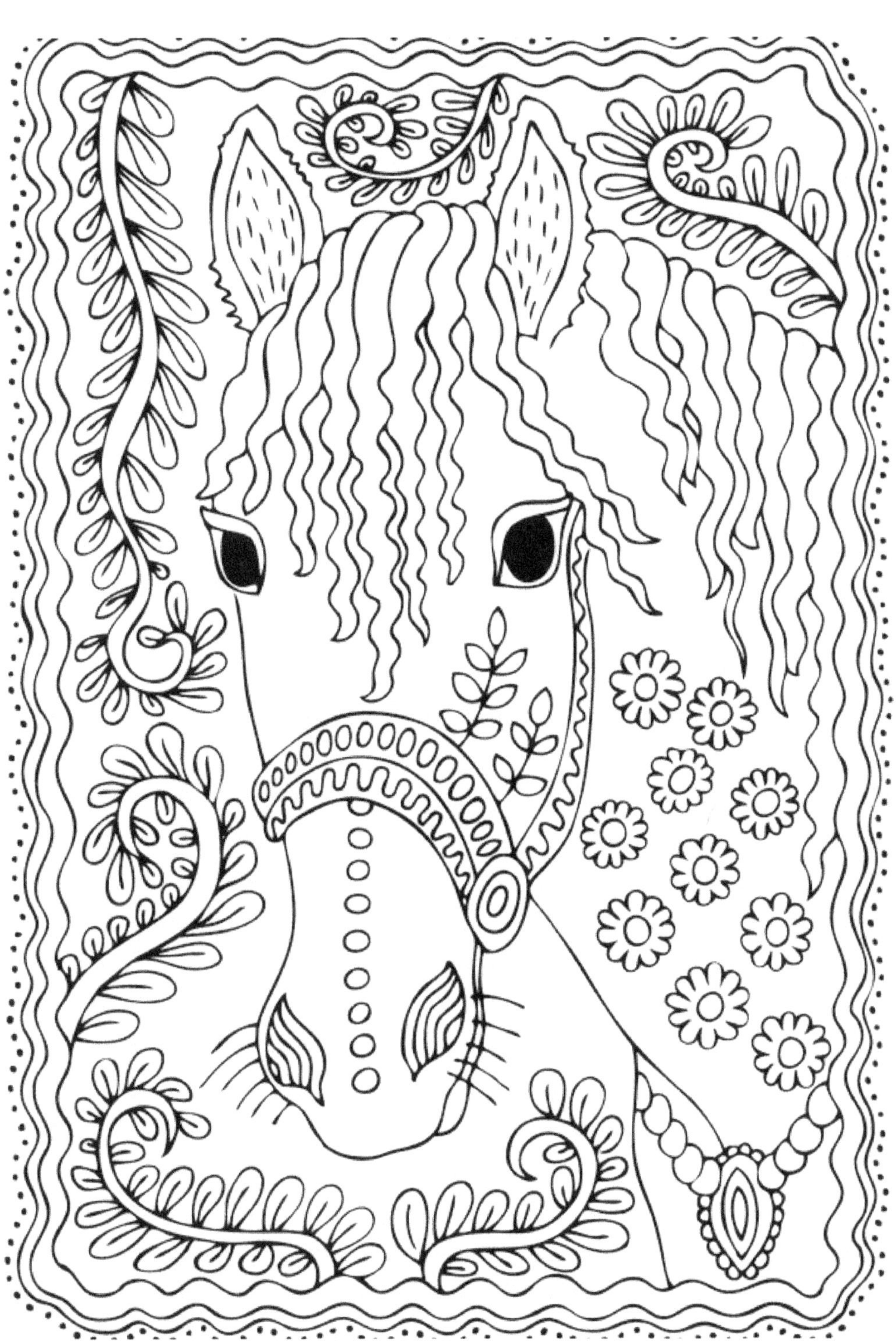

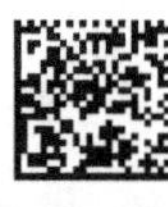